BRIGHT NOTES

THE BIRTH OF TRAGEDY AND OTHER WORKS BY FRIEDRICH NIETZSCHE

Intelligent Education

Nashville, Tennessee

BRIGHT NOTES: The Birth of Tragedy and Other Works
www.BrightNotes.com

No part of this publication may be used or reproduced in any manner whatsoever without written permission, except in the case of brief quotations in critical articles and reviews. For permissions, contact Influence Publishers http://www.influencepublishers.com.

ISBN: 978-1-645421-34-4 (Paperback)
ISBN: 978-1-645421-35-1 (eBook)

Published in accordance with the U.S. Copyright Office Orphan Works and Mass Digitization report of the register of copyrights, June 2015.

Originally published by Monarch Press.
Stanley V. McDaniel, 1965
2020 Edition published by Influence Publishers.

Interior design by Lapiz Digital Services. Cover Design by Thinkpen Designs.

Printed in the United States of America.

Library of Congress Cataloging-in-Publication Data forthcoming.
Names: Intelligent Education
Title: BRIGHT NOTES: The Birth of Tragedy and Other Works
Subject: SSTU004000 STUDY AIDS / Book Notes

CONTENTS

1) Introduction to Friedrich Nietzsche   1

2) The Birth of Tragedy   6

3) Textual Analysis
   - Essay 1   21
   - Essay 2   28
   - Essay 3   39

4) Introduction to Thus Spoke Zarathustra   50

5) Textual Analysis
   - Part 1   52
   - Part 2   76
   - Part 3   100
   - Part 4   116

6) Textual Analysis
   - Part 1   138
   - Part 2 - 5   155
   - Part 6 and 7   173
   - Part 8 and 9   184

7)	Essay Questions and Answers	197
8)	Bibliography	204
9)	Key to Important Passages	206

INTRODUCTION TO FRIEDRICH NIETZSCHE

Friedrich Nietzsche was born near Leipzig, Germany, on October 15, 1844. His father, who died of an injury before young Friedrich's sixth birthday, was a Lutheran pastor. The death of his father left him in the charge of his mother, his sister, and three other female relatives. The family moved from Roecken, the village of his birth, to Naumberg, where he attended a well-known school (the Pforta school) until 1864. He then entered Bonn University, and moved to Leipzig in 1865, where he studied philology. There he came under the influence of the German philosopher Arthur Schopenhauer (1788-1860), through the latter's book, *The World as Will and Idea*. Schopenhauer's view of the world is essentially a pessimistic one, and much of Nietzsche's later work was directed against this pessimism.

Nietzsche was an excellent student, and he received a teaching position in classical philology at Basle, Switzerland, in 1868, at the age of 24, before completing his doctorate. He remained in this post for ten years. For four of these years, he was an intimate friend of the composer Richard Wagner (1813-1883). This friendship came to an end, however, when Nietzsche rejected Wagner's return to religious sentiments, marked by the appearance of the opera Parsifal. The relationship with Wagner had a lasting effect upon Nietzsche's thought, and he was always interested in Wagner as a representative of the artistic temperament.

Nietzsche's first books were published during his employment at Basle. *The Birth of Tragedy* appeared in 1872, followed by *Untimely Meditations* (1873-76) and *Human, All Too Human* (1878-79), parts one and two. By the year 1879, his interest in philology as a primary topic had waned, although his linguistic study became incorporated into his philosophic technique. He was beset by illness, and he finally left his teaching post. His recovery was marked by the publication in 1880 of part three of *Human, All Too Human, and The Dawn* (1881). Nietzsche was convinced that the painful period of illness had refined and strengthened his insight and his intellectual skill. That this conceit was not unjustified is clearly shown by the remarkable surety with which he dissects contemporary society and anticipates future philosophical, psychological, and political developments.

In the years 1880-1889, Nietzsche wrote his well-known *Thus Spoke Zarathustra* (1883-85), as well as *The Gay Science* (1882-86), *Beyond Good and Evil* (1885-86), and *The Genealogy of Morals* (1887). *Ecce Homo*, an elaborate self-appraisal, and *The Antichrist*, a criticism of Christianity, were also written in this period, although they were published after 1890. His "last" work, *The Will to Power*, was never completed, but a collection of his notes was published under this title in 1904. In 1888, he again fell ill. After increasingly severe attacks of paralysis, he succumbed (August 25, 1900).

The four books treated in this Study Guide represent nearly the entire span of Nietzsche's creative life. *The Birth of Tragedy*, although primarily a discussion of the Greek tragic drama and the nature of art, presents several leading **themes** of his later work. Value, as a synthesis of the chaotic and the formal elements in life, and the continual recurrence of such synthesis, are among these themes. Here, also, he introduces his theory of tragic drama as a mingling of the "Dionysian" and the "Apollonian" - God-names which symbolize the dualism of the formless, active, and undifferentiated, on the one hand, and the formal "image" on the other.

The remaining three works are closely related. *Beyond Good and Evil* is an elaboration of some of the more obscure points in *Thus Spoke Zarathustra*, and *The Genealogy of Morals* is a detailed study of topics which appear in shorter form in *Beyond Good and Evil*, particularly the study of the ideals of asceticism and the notion of justice as punishment.

Because of the close relationship of these works, every attempt has been made to present cross-references, so that the student may correlate passages which deal with the same subject. This has been particularly the case in the "middle" book, *Beyond Good and Evil*, in which references to both the earlier and later volumes are given as often as possible. The prophetic character of Nietzsche's thought cannot be overlooked, and references are also given to modern works which bear upon the topic.

The four books differ greatly in form. The first and the last are the most continuous in structure. The two "middle" works are more artistic in character. *Zarathustra's* four parts are made up of short chapters, some of which reach high levels of poetic **metaphor**. However "loose" it may appear, however, the book actually has a high degree of artistic unity. Because it takes the form of a narrative of events in the life of Zarathustra, the action and the commentary have been kept separate, so that the "story line" may be followed more easily.

If any one conceptual "tool" is central in Nietzsche's philosophy, it is his rejection of "dualistic" interpretations of the world. Nietzsche was uncompromising in his belief that the understanding of the universe in terms of extreme opposites, such as those of "mind" and "body," was false. But his view is not monistic, in the sense that he accepts any one such element as "real" and rejects its opposite (this would still be a tacit acceptance of irreconcilable opposites). Instead, he asserted the possibility of a development of one extreme out of the other, contradicting the "prejudice" that nothing can arise out of its opposite. Nietzsche's position is, as a result, extremely close to that of the American philosopher John Dewey, who held to a "principle of continuity" and whose conviction that the highest intellectual functions are developmentally related to the lowest organic behavior parallels Nietzsche's conception of the will to power as a biological law.

This same rejection of dualism is given a less psychological (but no less vehement) expression in the philosophy of the contemporary British thinker Gilbert Ryle, whose book, *The Concept of Mind*, is an elaborate polemic against the separation of mind and body. Nietzsche carried his own rejection of "opposites" into the field of human intercourse, affirming, for example, that friendship and enmity are closely related, that justice and criminality are reciprocal, and that the highest spiritual values may even derive their worth from the deepest sensuality. His own account of the "prejudice of opposites" is to be found in chapter one of *Beyond Good and Evil*. It is strongly recommended that this chapter, "Prejudices of Philosophers," be read prior to the study of *Thus Spoke Zarathustra*.

In general, Nietzsche expresses himself in brief passages, many of which say the same thing in a slightly different way. In order to facilitate study, a *Key to Important Passages* has been included in this Study Guide, which correlates the main sections in which six of Nietzsche's most characteristic views are discussed: the Superman, the Will to Power, Eternal Recurrence, Self-overcoming, Reality and Knowledge, and Nihilism. The headings in the discussion of *The Birth of Tragedy* have been introduced for the student's convenience; they are not, however, present in the original work. They have been introduced to make the task of organization and reference easier.

Nietzsche was a literary as well as philosophical genius, and it is not entirely possible to convey, in a Study Guide of this nature, the depth of mood and range of expression which is to be found in the original. It is hoped, therefore, that the student will also consult the actual texts, in order to "feel" Nietzsche's ideas in their original setting. A bibliography has been included for this purpose.

THE BIRTH OF TRAGEDY

APOLLO AND DIONYSOS

The development of art is the result of a constant interplay between two contending elements in the creative life of man: the Apollonian and the Dionysian. These terms are taken from the names of two gods of ancient Greece, Apollo, the god of prophecy and patron of the arts, and Dionysos, the god of wine and the vineyards. Nietzsche views these two mythical figures as the personifications of opposing creative tendencies in man. By constant opposition, each stimulates the other to further effort, and the result is the growth of art. But the two tendencies also have a certain dependency upon one another, and in the Greek tragedy, a form of staged drama which was widely popular in ancient Greece, a balance of the two tendencies was achieved.

DREAM AND INTOXICATION

The Apollonian tendency is closely related to dreaming. Dreaming, says Nietzsche, is a means of interpreting life through images. The dreamer, the image-maker, takes a deep delight in the myriad forms and shapes of the dream images, which are not perceived by the intellect, but by the artistic (aesthetic) sense. An essential part of the experience of dreams is an ever-present realization that the images are not real, but illusory. Nietzsche calls this the "fair illusion of the dream sphere." Apollo represents the arts in which images are deliberately produced as an interpretation of existence. These are called the plastic arts, such as painting and sculpture. Such images, however, must always preserve the feeling of illusion, or they will fail in preserving artistic quality, presenting instead merely "crass reality." Thus the Apollonian tendency is the tendency to impose form and order upon the world. Nietzsche, in consequence, refers to Apollo as representing a principle of individuation, by which he means a principle which separates elements of a fluctuating world into individual units and places them in ordered, understandable relation to each other. Dionysos, on the other hand, represents the destruction of individuality. Physical intoxication is analogous to the "glorious transport" of "Dionysiac rapture." The Dionysiac state is one in which the boundaries between individuals are destroyed. In it, a sense of mystical unity with the universe is experienced. The universe itself is seen to be a unity, a "one." Seized by the Dionysian spirit, an individual abandons the social veneer of intellectual rules, and "forgets himself completely." Dionysos represents, then the overpowering urges of a primitive response to the coming of spring - an uninhibited, free, and direct communion with the deep mysteries of nature which defy formal understanding, and to which all images stand opposed as Apollonian illusion to the Dionysian reality.

THE ARTIST

Every artist, as an artist, seeks to represent these moods in an artistic medium. The poets who were the authors of Greek tragedy unified both elements. An image which succeeds in expressing "complete oneness with the essence of the universe" would be at once an Apollonian and a Dionysian artistic triumph. The Greeks were able to control Dionysian urges through an intense worship of Apollonian form in art. Nietzsches contrasts them with "Dionysiac barbarians" who, imitating the Satyrs (servants of Dionysos devoted to sensual pleasure), allowed themselves to be overcome in celebrations of wild and unrestrained revelry. But even for the Greeks, Dionysos is not subdued, but only pacified. In the "treaty" that bound the two forces to respect each other, Nietzsche sees "the most important event in the history of Greek ritual." As long as the basically destructive Dionysian force can express itself in the form of an Apollonian image, a sense of deep reality may be achieved without the risk of losing all anchors and being cast adrift in a terrifying maelstrom.

WISDOM OF DIONYSOS

Nietzsche relates the legendary answer of Silenus, a companion of Dionysos, to King Midas. Upon being asked what was the greatest good of man, Silenus replied, "What would be best for you is quite beyond your reach: not to have been born, not to be, to be nothing. But the second best is to die soon." In this reply, Silenus expresses the Dionysian truth that existence in the form of an individual is a painful thing, because individuality is at root an illusion and must be supported by illusions. Dionysian reality, opposed to illusion, is nonrational, and no individual can survive, as an individual, within it.

THE OLYMPIAN GODS

Nietzsche comes to the conclusion that the Greeks, keenly aware of the pain of existence, were forced to create the mythical world of the gods in order to live at all. The gods "justified human life by living it themselves." The Greeks saw the gods as images of themselves, much as one sees oneself mirrored in a dream, while still aware that the image is not really oneself, but rather a "fair illusion." By means of such illusion, the Greeks withstood their suffering. Such "illusion," whether in dream, myth, or art, need not be pleasant. What matters most is the presence of form and control over the basically irrational and uncontrolled nature of the universe.

GREEK NATURALISM

The Greeks were not in a simple state of rapturous harmony with nature, as some, such as Rousseau (a famous eighteenth-century French thinker), may have thought. The Greek connection with nature was complex, not simple. It was born out of the connection between art and pain.

BEAUTY IN ART

Beauty is not to be found in mere imitation of nature, but in a successful imposition of Apollonian form upon the primitive Dionysian urge. In true beauty, pain and joy blend into one: "... in every exuberant joy there is an undertone of terror."

Nietzsche speaks of Beauty as a kind of redemption. It is a "redemption through illusion," in which an individual comes to know himself. Apollo "demands self-control" and awareness of the limits of the individual will. The constant onslaught of the Dionysian, under which the individual may lose himself completely, demands a repeated renewal of self-awareness. Thus Greek art, with its emphasis upon form, rhythm, and harmony, is not a sign of the absence of Dionysos, but rather a bastion of defense against his constant presence. Greek art, he says, is like "a perpetual military encampment ... against the titanic and barbaric menace of Dionysos."

ARTISTIC OBJECTIVITY

Yet knowledge of self through art is not a sign that art is purely personal and subjective. Rather, art stimulates a renewal of self, a reconstruction of form after each attack by the self-destroying Dionysian force. All is lost in art, if it is interpreted as mere subjective expression of personal will. Art demands a "triumph over personal will and desire," and must embody "objectivity and disinterested contemplation." The true artist must go through a Dionysiac phase, in which he rejects personal feelings and becomes "identified with the original oneness." Only those Apollonian images which arise in reaction to the pain of losing oneself are artistic in the true sense.

WORLD JUSTIFICATION

Tragedy, the highest expression of true art as an Apollonian-Dionysian combination, is not only a "**metaphysical** solace," an illusion necessary to sustain life; it is a means of interpreting the world as an artistic product. Only as such, Nietzsche claims, can the world be "justified." Later in the text, Nietzsche repeats this view, and appears to mean that true art justifies the world in the sense that it makes the "horror of existence" bearable. (See the comments at the end of the chapter.)

THE SPIRIT OF MUSIC

Folk song, says Nietzsche, is a reflection of a preponderance of Dionysian feelings. Evidence for this is that folk song values melody over text. This corresponds to a valuation of the generative but formless factor, represented by Dionysos, over any particular form. One might look at folk song as an expression of a universal will which takes now this form, now another, without losing its Dionysian undercurrents. As Nietzsche puts it, "melody gives birth to poetry again and again."

Folk poetry is an attempt to "imitate" music by means of language. There are two kinds of poetry: that which imitates the Apollonian world of apparent form, and that which imitates the musical world of Dionysian reality. The impulse to interpret music in terms of images-for example, to "picture" a Beethoven symphony as representing country scenery-is a manifestation of the same desire as that of the poet who seeks to create a music of words.

Music is thus opposed to the plastic arts as Dionysos is opposed to Apollo. It is "independent of image or concept." It refers to "primordial contradiction and pain," and "symbolizes a sphere which is both earlier than appearance and beyond it." Language, on the other hand, is the instrument of Apollo and of the intellect. It cannot tolerate contradiction, and thus can never succeed fully in imitating the spirit of music.

STRUCTURE OF TRAGIC DRAMA

In the Greek tragic plays, there is a chorus of speakers positioned between the audience and the players. Historically, tragedy began with the chorus alone, the acting out of the drama being added later. Nietzsche finds in this structure a clue to his interpretation of tragedy as a blending of the Apollonian and Dionysian forces.

He rejects certain other ideas regarding the function of the chorus, for example, that it is a reflection of a desire for constitutional democracy, or that the chorus represents an "ideal spectator" - a view attributed to the German critic A. W. Schlegel. Nietzsche is more in sympathy with the poet Schiller's view that the chorus serves to separate the play from reality ... a necessary condition for preserving the "fair illusion" of true art.

Nietzsche expands this view by means of his twofold conception of art. The chorus, he suggests, is that Dionysian force which generates the imagery upon the stage. The formal stage play becomes seen, through the eyes of the chorus, as an Apollonian interpretation of the reality which the chorus symbolizes for the spectator. The chorus affords the spectator the opportunity to enter into the selfless condition of a multitude, without identifying with the actors, which would destroy the artistic illusion. Nietzsche says, "the stage with its action was originally conceived as pure vision and ... the only reality was the chorus, who created that vision out of itself ... it proclaims a truth that issues from the heart of the world." Thus the structure of tragedy reflects the twofold division of verse mentioned earlier: there is, on the one hand, the musical "Dionysian poetry of the chorus," and on the other, the "Apollonian dream world of the scene."

THE INTERPRETATION OF MYTH

Through the musical Dionysian force, Nietzsche continues, Greek myth became transformed; in the drama, myth assumed a higher meaning and came to express the Dionysian wisdom of Silenus. The hero of the tragic stage represents the god Dionysos; the suffering of the hero is a symbolic form of the suffering which must accompany individuation, which is represented by the god's momentary dramatic form. He appears on the stage, as Nietzsche says, "enmeshed in the web of individual will."

The Dionysian wisdom has a positive side: the anticipation of a return to the original "oneness" of the universe. Nietzsche recalls the myth of the sorrowing Demeter (goddess of the Earth's produce, mother of Proserpine), in which Demeter "rejoiced only when she was told that she might once again bear Dionysos." Nietzsche sees in this a "profound and mystic wisdom," the knowledge that all existence is one, and that separation of the one into individuals is an evil. Art, he says, is the symbol of the hope that Dionysos will return, and the "spell of individuation" broken.

THE DECLINE OF TRAGEDY

Greek tragic drama began to decline when the all-important requirement that the action on the stage must be separated from real life was abandoned. The poet Euripides (480-406 B.C.) exemplifies this change. **Realism** on the stage at once destroys the separating influence of the chorus, and the objective point of view of the spectator, which, as we have seen, Nietzsche regarded as essential to the tragic art. Nietzsche says that "Euripides succeeded in transporting the spectator onto the stage."

THE TWO SPECTATORS

What was the reason for this change? Nietzsche attributes it to the arrival of a new factor in Greek life: the intellectual spirit of inquiry, the desire for knowledge in all things. Euripides, says Nietzsche, did not judge drama from the point of view of the mass of spectators, as some have thought. But there were two spectators whose voices he heeded. The first of these was Euripides himself-Euripides as a thinker. Euripides as thinker, rather than as poet, observed that in contrast to the apparent outward simplicity of the earlier tragic drama (as represented by the poet Aeschylus), there were a host of hidden meanings which remained unclear to him. In particular, the function of the chorus, the ambiguous solutions of moral problems, the treatment of classic mythology, and the "irregular distribution of fortune and misfortune" were difficult to understand. As Nietzsche puts it, "the clearest figure trailed after it a comet's tail which seemed to point to ... something that could not be wholly elucidated."

Euripides, finding the lack of clarity disturbing, and believing that the light of reason should illuminate all important things, turned to a new voice in Greek life: the powerful inquiring spirit of the philosopher Socrates. This famous thinker, then, was the "second spectator". In Socrates, the logical side of man had become exaggerated. He stands at the opposite pole from that of the thoroughgoing mystic, in whom the instinctual side is supreme. Socrates the man, almost as one possessed, serves as a spokesman for the rational nature of man. He represents a rational optimism which declares that all things can and must be known. His watchword is that "virtue is knowledge."

All that is obscure in drama is best left alone, in the Socratic view. This drove poetry to find new forms of expression. The works of Socrates' pupil, Plato, were the first example of a new art form, the novel, in which poetry takes a back seat to explanation. This same tendency is found in the drama of Euripides, in the form of an introductory prologue, which attempts to make clear the action of the play. The tendency to **realism**, in which the spectator is "transported onto the stage," is a part of this attempt to make the drama more understandable. Finally, the chorus, whose place should be uppermost, was looked upon as a mere remnant of a less-developed period in history. Thus, under the influence of the Socratic emphasis upon reason, tragedy begins its decline. The optimism of reason is the death of tragedy.

POSITIVE INFLUENCE OF SOCRATES

Emphasis upon critical reason as a pathway to truth, which Socrates symbolizes for all future ages, has a special restorative power for art. The creed of Socrates was that reason alone can justify existence, by making it understood. It is, thus, optimistic, because it places a faith in reason which reaches to the limits of all things, But, according to Nietzsche, this optimism is unwarranted, because existence, as he has said before, is basically irrational and contradictory. Logic, the bulwark of reason, can never lead the human mind to the ultimate secrets of all things.

Comment

As Nietzsche said earlier, language (from which logic springs) can never reach the limits of the Dionysian "primordial contradiction." This view, that language, logic, and reason produce in the end only a disappointment in false hopes is also a mark of many present-day philosophers and writers of the school called "existentialism."

When the inquiring mind finally realizes this fundamental limitation of reason, it is seized by a feeling of the tragic-a pessimism which overcomes optimistic conviction - and seeks the only remedy possible, "the remedy of art." Thus art is reborn, and its supremacy recognized; it is indeed the only true justification of existence.

THE REBIRTH OF TRAGEDY

Nietzsche now turns to a defense of his thesis that tragedy is born out of music, and that the decline of true music is the decline of tragedy as well. Both music and images are abstract, but music is an abstract expression of the "heart of man." Concepts and images, on the other hand, are the abstract forms of perceptions, or the "outer shell" of things. Only music can give deep significance to images. If the spirit of music is distorted by misguided attempts to imitate the outer world of perception (as in "program" music), the significance of art is lost.

The modern world is entranced by the Socratic idea. This anti-Dionysian, or "Alexandrian," culture idolizes "the man of theory." In music, the Alexandrian-Socratic culture is represented by opera, with its emphasis on the text over the music. But there are signs that modern man is becoming uncomfortably aware of the limits of such a culture. Some geniuses, such as the philosophers Kant and Schopenhauer, have challenged the idea that science is the last word in all things. When this pessimism overcomes the optimism of reason, a new tragic age will begin. The music of the great German composers Bach, Beethoven, and Wagner signals the renewal of Dionysian art. In a characteristically impassioned outburst, Nietzsche invokes the new age:

"But what amazing change is wrought in that gloomy desert of our culture by the wand of Dionysos! All that is half-alive, rotten, broken and stunted the whirlwind wraps in a red cloud of dust and carries off like a vulture. Our distracted eyes look for all that has vanished and are confused, for what they see has risen from beneath the earth into the golden light, so full and green, so richly alive. In the midst of all this life, joy, and sorrow, tragedy sits in noble ecstasy, listening to a sad, distant song which tells of the mothers of being, whose names are Wish, Will, Woe."

GREEK CIVILIZATION AND TRAGEDY

Strong patriotism is dependent upon a positive attitude toward individuality. Such an attitude is not supported by the Dionysian spirit, but is a natural result of the Apollonian. Either of these conditions, if the other is excluded, leads to a weakness in the political state. India represents a state in which exaggeration of the Dionysian spirit has led to a near-complete denial of the secular world. Rome, where Apollo held sway, represented a total secularization and a consequent loss of creativity. Greek culture, through the medicine of the tragedy, attained greatness by coming to an ideal balance between the creative Dionysian force and the Apollonian stability. However, the symbol and heart of this balance-tragedy-requires a universal cultural myth. It is through myth, a shared and common Apollonian device, that the Dionysian creative musical spirit can be felt deeply and yet controlled. Tragic myth is "Dionysian wisdom made concrete through Apollonian artifice." Without myth, Apollonian control of the creative forces is scattered and "rambling."

THE MODERN DILEMMA

As tragedy disappears, so does myth. But any civilization without myth must lose also its creativity. The present day, with its lack of unifying myth, is the result of the destructive side of Socratic doctrine. Modern man stands spiritually naked and starving, forced to grasp at any bit of flotsam which will sustain his need for deeper roots. A nation must be able to relate its daily endeavors to something beyond, an eternal source.

That very same element in tragedy which Euripides found so disturbing, the external clarity opposed to an internal twilight of deeper significance, is thus the very symbol of the need of modern man. No mere "pleasant" art, designed to divert the senses momentarily from the problems of life, can be enough. The tragic content of myth, the "ugliness and disharmony," conveys the supreme aesthetic conviction that the world is justified even though it is a world of pain and suffering. Thus Nietzsche concludes with an affirmation of his doctrine that only through art, and tragic art above all, can existence gain that deeper meaning which glorifies a culture and at the same time strengthens the life of the individual with an ever-renewing, creative significance.

Comment

Clarifying the meaning of Nietzsche's main notions - the Apollonian and the Dionysian - is not an easy matter. Speaking of them as "gods" is a strong literary device, but it does not aid our understanding. How, for example, is one to tell, of a particular work of art, whether or not it possesses a "balance" of the two factors? To begin with, it is not clear whether the Dionysian" and the "Apollonian" are things located in the work of art (as are the form and the matter of the work), or in the artist's method, or in his goals, or in the effect on the spectator, or in all or just some of these. The very fact they are referred to by many different terms, such as "factors," "elements," and "tendencies" indicates that it is not quite clear just what they stand for. It is true that in every human endeavor, there is some uncertainty. No one knows exactly what hidden aspects of his own personality, habits, and adaptability may come into play in the process of reaching a desired, goal. On the other hand, no endeavor is properly called such, unless an element of regularity and of form, rule, and learned habit is called upon. In this sense, both Dionysian (uncertainty) and Apollonian (regularity) are always present, and true newness depends upon their interplay. But such an interpretation of Nietzsche's meaning would be much too shallow, even if helpful. One must look elsewhere for assistance.

In seeking further illumination, one may go either forward or backward, historically speaking. There are many hints of Nietzsche's thought, some of them exciting and tantalizing, in the writings of the Greek philosophers prior to Socrates, when philosophy was just beginning to emerge from myth. The writings of these men, such as Thales, Heraclitus, and Anaxagoras, have received interesting interpretations by the British author F. M. Cornford, who has also translated and commented upon the works of Plato. The German philosopher Hegel (1770-1831), with his doctrine of historical evolution through the interaction of opposing forces, has always been considered a great influence upon Nietzsche. More significant with regard to Nietzsche's insight and depth of thought are the writings of Sigmund Freud and Carl Jung, whose psychological theories contain many elements closely related to Nietzsche's viewpoint. Some, indeed, take the position that Nietzsche is of greater significance as a psychologist than as a philosopher.

There is, however, another side of the picture, which places Nietzsche indisputably in the ranks of the philosophers. In the introductory passage titled "a critical backward glance," written some fourteen years after the book was published, Nietzsche states that his main question was one of "the value placed on existence." He was deeply impressed by the thought that moral values - those values supposedly derived either from the supernatural dictates of religion, or from an ultimate knowledge of "the good" - were insufficient to sustain and justify human existence. The new evolutionary, biological view of man was undercutting a supernatural sanction for moral values, and knowledge alone, as Nietzsche believed, cannot reach to the limits of all human experience, even though this was the hope of Socratic optimism.

Nietzsche, therefore, was seeking a new justification for existence, or a new basis for ultimate values. He suggests in *The Birth of Tragedy* that it is to be found in art, and in the continual renewal of art. Although this is a **theme** which he later rejected, the problem which led to it - the problem of the justification of values in the absence of religion or of ultimate knowledge - dominates his thought to the very end. To say that certain major tendencies in modern philosophy, such as pragmatism and existentialism, share this concern, would not be an exaggeration. In this respect Nietzsche sets the stage in many ways for the unfolding of modern thought.

THE GENEALOGY OF MORALS

TEXTUAL ANALYSIS

ESSAY 1

PREFACE

Nietzsche introduces his subject: the investigation of the origin and value of morality. While he does not define "morality," he speaks of "these values," mentioning specifically only the values of compassion, self-denial, and self-sacrifice, which he calls "instincts." Regarding the basis for appraising these values, he speaks of their "intrinsic worth," which includes the degree to which they "promote" and "benefit" mankind.

Comment

In the last part of the first essay (part 17), Nietzsche discusses this again, saying that the "worth" of a table of values is measured with respect to some goal, and that this worth will vary according to the goal-for example, the well-being of the greatest number, or the good of the aristocracy.

FIRST ESSAY

1-8. Nietzsche begins with a scathing criticism of a school of "English psychologists" whose theory, he says, is that moral sentiments arise out of the appreciation of useful habits, where the original reason for valuing these habits (that is, their utility) has been forgotten. He dislikes this theory because it suggests that morality arises out of a passive acceptance of traditional patterns of action, and because it supposes that men can forget things which have every reason to be remembered - the usefulness of certain beneficial actions. He is more sympathetic toward the view of Herbert Spencer (1820-1903), who believed that the useful and the good are identical, without supposing that any lapse of memory is involved. But Nietzsche feels that value judgments are not, in fact, based upon consideration of the useful, but rather upon the relation of a "ruling class" to a lower, servant class.

Nietzsche is here concerned with the meaning of the pair of words "good" and "bad"; this pair of words has a different meaning than the pair "good" and "evil." In the former case, "good" is associated with the concept of the noble class, and "bad" is associated with the concept of the peasant class. That this association is historically correct is borne out by the history of language and the relations between words; for instance, in German the word for "bad" is schlecht, and the word for "simple" (i.e., peasantlike) is schlicht, and for a time, these terms were used interchangeably. Nietzsche warns against the "democratic prejudice" that may prevent an unbiased view of his thesis. He says that the Greek noble class applied to themselves the word esthlos, which connotes a person who is "true." The Latin word for "good," bonus, he traces to an earlier word meaning "warrior." His hypothesis, then, is that the ruling class is also thought of as a class of the highest spiritual or divine qualities, and that the connection between words for "good" and words for the ruling class is a partial support for this idea. Originally, he holds, "good" and "bad" were terms for different social classes.

Nietzsche next considers the case in which the ruling class is made up of priests. Here, the words "pure" and "impure" may also occur as words distinguishing the higher from the lower class, even though the "pure" man may simply be one who follows set rules for bodily cleanliness and health. A priest-aristocracy, says Nietzsche, maintains a value system which is quite different from that which would be maintained by a warrior-aristocracy. Health, strength, beauty, power, and a love of life and the adventurous in life - these are the values of the latter. In contrast, the priest-aristocracy inverts these values and says that the weak, the poor, the suffering, and the ugly are the truly "good" people. In addition, adventure and chance are looked upon as evil. Nietzsche attributes this slave morality to the Jews.

Comment

Here we meet with the distinction good/evil (as opposed to the distinction good/bad). The "bad," to the ruling class, is simply an undesirable state of being; but the "evil," to the priest-aristocracy, is more than that-it is a way of life to be condemned, and the man who lives according to the "warrior" standards is subject to moral condemnation-he is guilty, he is sinful. These adjectives do not apply to mere "badness," which simply means "belonging to the lower class."

This slave morality, Nietzsche continues, arose out of vengeance and hatred (directed against the warrior-aristocracy). From this root, he says, grew the tree of Christian love and redemption. Nietzsche interprets the martyrdom of Christ as a "bait," which, with its hypnotic appeal, was meant to draw the whole world into an acceptance of the slave morality, assuring the victory of the priestly value system.

9-12. The ethical system based upon the values of the priest-aristocracy is now firmly entrenched. What are its primary characteristics? It is not a noble morality, because it grew out of the irritations which accompany impotence-out of "rancor." As such, it is not affirmative and active, but emphasizes negation and passivity. It is passive, because it originates as a reaction to an external, hostile group. It emphasizes humility rather than nobility. Contrasting views of happiness bring out the difference between the two value systems. The warrior-aristocracy finds happiness in action, but the priest-aristocracy finds it in passive inaction, represented by the concept of the "Sabbath." Similarly, a high value is placed upon intellectual pursuits by the priest-aristocracy, in contrast to the active orientation of the nobles, who view intellectual pursuits with a certain degree of suspicion.

The most important difference is closely allied to these; it stems from the repression of emotions, which characterizes the priestly morality. This repression, a storing up of feelings of envy and resentment, works like a poison in the psychology of the individual, and requires strong "priestly cures" (which never really "cure"). On the other hand, the emotions of resentment are purged from the noble man by spontaneous activity, which is not condemned in his value system.

The basis of the slave morality is the notion of "evil," as all that characterizes the enemy (the nobility). The notion of "good" grows out of this, as the negation of the evil. But the process is reversed in the case of the noble (warrior) class. There, the notion of "good" comes first, and "bad" arises in contrast to the "good." The idea of the "bad" is only secondary and incidental to the positive morality of the nobles; but the notion of evil is primary in the value system of the priest-aristocracy. It is true that the active morality of the nobles is a thing to inspire fear; beastly instincts, as well as creative ones, are always potentially at hand. But it is better, Nietzsche believes, to face this than to open the door to psychological degeneracy, which the repressive slave morality encourages. His main objection to the slave morality is that it appears to signify a failure on the part of man to find value in himself; it joins a fear of man with a loss of love for, and faith in, man (and in life in general). This is the nihilism that Nietzsche deplores.

13-15. The basic logic of the slave morality, Nietzsche says, need not be questioned. "Good" is defined as the opposite of evil, and evil is identified with the strong and the noble, the warriors, and all of their main character traits. This reasoning, in itself, is not "incorrect" in any absolute sense of the word. But a peculiar inversion of logic occurs when the strong are called to account for their behavior, when they are taken to be "guilty" of their manifestations of strength. Here, he holds, it is necessary to suppose that the strong can do otherwise, that they can help what they do. In order to support this supposition, the idea of a "free subject" arises; a "soul," or a part of the mind which is wholly responsible for all outward acts, and therefore is the cause of these acts. But supposing this, Nietzsche believes, is a mistaken reversal of cause and effect. It takes a cause (the spontaneous activity of the strong individual) to be an effect of the action of some mysterious "neutral agent." Natural science, he continues, committed a similar error in inventing "energy" as a cause for the motion of material objects, instead of defining it as equivalent to such motion. The free-willing "soul" as a cause of actions, and therefore as something which can be blamed for them, is as unreal as this prescientific "energy." (See *Beyond Good and Evil*, sections 12 and 17-19.)

Now Nietzsche enumerates, in the course of an imaginary dialogue, those values which he identifies with the priest-aristocracy and slave morality: kindness, humility, obedience, patience, forgiveness, "loving one's enemy," and the triumph of justice. He does not condemn these sentiments as such. It is their foundation and their use which he dislikes. They are, he says, mere transformations of the feelings of impotence, submission, and cowardice which mark the slave class. A primary example of this is that idea of justice which is based upon vengeance. If such values are to be noble, they must be nobly motivated, not founded upon the repression of inadequacies.

Comment

This is in accordance with the many references in *Thus Spoke Zarathustra* to benevolent acts which arise out of the spontaneous overflow of life from a strong personality. Nietzsche is not against kindness and forgiveness as such, but he is against their being no more than a disguised form of cowardice and reprisal. He rejects the dictum, "Thou shalt be kind," in favor of the affirmation, "I will be kind, but I reserve the right to be otherwise."

Nietzsche summarizes his position. There is a conflict between the two value frameworks, "good-bad" and "good-evil." The latter has been uppermost in recent times. He traces this struggle historically as a conflict between "Rome" and "Israel." The re-emergence of interest in Greek classicism, and the advent of Napoleon, are instances of the continuing (but isolated) life of the "good-bad" system. Nietzsche concludes this essay by pointing out that the title of his earlier book, *Beyond Good and Evil*, did not indicate a complete denial of morality, as some might think. By "beyond good and evil," he did not mean "beyond good and bad."

THE GENEALOGY OF MORALS

TEXTUAL ANALYSIS

ESSAY 2

SECOND ESSAY

1-3. This essay deals with the notions of "guilt" and "bad conscience." Man, Nietzsche says, is unique because he has become able to claim the right to make promises. Such a right presupposes the ability to keep promises. What is remarkable in this ability is that it, in turn, presupposes a continuity of purpose and of memory throughout a period of time, and there is a strong natural tendency to forget, which opposes this ability. This opposing faculty of shutting out past events is a sign of health, since it helps to destroy the effect of past failures and discomforts, making the present more bearable and the future more hopeful. A man who is unable to forget, Nietzsche says, is a sick man.

Against this power to forget, there stands the ability to remember; not simply a passive retention of impressions, but an active memory, which means an ability to maintain a purpose over a period of time, and to return to it after interruptions. This active memory is a "memory of the will." In order to maintain purpose in this manner, man must be able to predict and control his own behavior to a certain extent. Such a man, he says, has made himself "calculable."

Comment

Philosophers sometimes distinguish "habit memory" from "memory of facts." Many animals have varying degrees of habit memory, and are able to carry through, to a successful conclusion, complex endeavors which require a continuity of purpose. The industry and perseverance of beavers is an example of this. However, man seems to be unique in his ability to enter deliberately upon a course of training which will terminate in an ability which is predictable, such as learning to play a musical instrument. He can make himself "calculable" in a great variety of ways. In addition, he is able to anticipate his future behavior consciously, that is, he is able to communicate it to others. This communication of what is calculable is what is essential to the making of promises. (See also *Beyond Good and Evil*, sections 188-189 and the Comment following.)

Social custom is one of the primary factors in rendering man "calculable." Promises can be made within the social context, because behavior under the force of custom is predictable to a high degree. But the ultimate end of the tendency to become calculable is the autonomous individual, one who renders himself calculable through self-discipline and knowledge of himself, and not through the externally imposed device of social rules. The autonomous man, in contrast to the moral man, does not keep promises because of the customary morality-he is free from that morality-but because he has promised. Such a man is superior, and is in fact the goal of mankind.

Comment

Nietzsche does not give convincing reasons for considering the "autonomous man" as superior to others. He asserts that others will fear and respect such a man, and that he will have mastery over others because he has mastered himself. But a man is not superior (at least in some senses of the word) simply because he can command others, and it is not ever certain that it is true that all who master themselves can command others. However, Nietzsche does suggest that such a man possesses a "scale of values," and this is a clue to his view that the autonomous man is superior. He is more healthy and more creative, and if health and creativity are high values, then he is, in this sense at least, superior. It should be noticed that Nietzsche is here carrying through his persistent **theme** that moral qualities, such as keeping promises, should come from within each individual, in the form of a creative affirmation of the individual will, and not as an obligation performed out of fear of reprisal in the form of social condemnation, God's will, or pangs of guilt.

The instinct to obey his self-imposed responsibility, on the part of the autonomous man, is called conscience. Nietzsche believes that conscience, as a free, instinctive compulsion to carry out responsibility, is a hard-won faculty. Man remembers best, he says, that which hurts the most. Therefore societies have taken drastic means to instill the promise-keeping habit. Sacrifices, pledges, cruel rituals, and stringent laws which decree tortures and death. Asceticism, a self-imposed austere way of life, is one of these means by which the individual impresses upon himself the importance of "following the rules".

4-7. Nietzsche defines bad conscience as an awareness of one's own guilt (to which he later adds the descriptive terms "remorse" and "a moral pang"). He now begins a lengthy discourse designed to show that bad conscience does not arise out of fear of punishment. Punishment, he says, was not originally associated with guilt, but with indebtedness. The purpose of inflicting punishment was to provide for the payment of a debt or damage incurred. In early societies, an actual contract may have been drawn up, in which the debtor promises to suffer pain, indignities, or even death, if he does not keep his part of the bargain. In these cases, a fairly detailed table of equivalences between amount owed and the magnitude of pain to be inflicted may have been consulted. Punishment, therefore, originated as a part of relations of trade and business, or at least in connection with the exchange of possessions.

The reasons that punishment was able to serve the purpose of repayment of debts is that the infliction of pain upon another gives pleasure, which is valuable in itself. Such pleasure, he says, is a manifestation of the desire for power; it is a natural accompaniment of that desire fulfilled.

Comment

If this seems a strange or hard doctrine, it must be remembered that Nietzsche is treating the subject historically. Even today, however, a close observation of crowd behavior at boxing matches or the scene of an accident may make his point seem less harsh. However, the fact that people may take pleasure in observing the pain of another, even if true without qualification, is not equivalent to the thesis that receipt of such pleasure constituted an alternate form for payment of debts. Nietzsche himself says that he is merely making "a suggestion," and admits that the matter may be too complex and lost in history to be fully explained. His main point is that punishment is associated with payment, not necessarily with moral transgression.

In connection with his general idea that punishment was originally a form of payment, and that its value (as such) arose out of the pleasure it provided the creditor, Nietzsche makes several further points: (1) Life is not necessarily "better" these days, when pleasure in inflicting pain is looked down upon and repressed, because to a certain extent our natural instincts are less free than they were before. (2) Pain itself appears to have been of less importance, or more bearable, in primitive societies, than it is today. (3) The instinct which permits man to take a certain amount of pleasure from the pain of others is not wholly eradicated, even today, but merely given less objectionable forms ("sublimated"). (4) The idea of an "all-seeing" divinity may have come, in part, from the desire to render all suffering meaningful, that is, by supplying an ever-present spectator (the divinity) who is a witness to even the most private pain. (5) From the point of view of a "spectator" God, the need for variety, for the unexpected, may have led Greek philosophers to "invent" man's free will, as a necessary element of uncertainty which would provide the variety required.

8-10. Sentiments of guilt and obligation arose out of the economic relationships of purchase and payment which are to be found in all primitive societies. The crudest form of justice consists of the idea of the proper payment of obligations and the keeping of contracts. Because people are, in a sense, indebted to the community itself for their well-being and livelihood, a second form of justice arises, the idea of repayment to the community, through punishment received, for any acts which may endanger the public unity. A criminal may be looked upon as one who, in violating the laws which preserve the autonomy of the group, becomes a debtor to the state. Punishment is the means of obtaining payment, and the demand for payment is a just demand. Justice consists in payment of what is owed to the community by a transgressor (one who goes against the laws of the group).

A third stage is reached as the community becomes more secure and capable of sustaining itself regardless of individual transgressions. In this stage, punishment fades into the background, and an elaborate system of laws "fixes the price" for varying offenses. Here, justice is done when the price is paid, and the offender himself is not marked as a particularly "bad" man. A legal means is supplied through which he can pay for his crime without having to suffer excessive condemnation or complete rejection by the group. This inclination to make it easier for the offender, which is a sign of the strong and secure community, may be carried into a fourth stage, in which offenders are simply "let off" for minor crimes. At this stage, justice becomes "self-canceling," and Nietzsche calls this "mercy," which he says is a luxury of the strong.

Comment

A look at our present legal system, in which traffic violations, for example, are not considered as a matter of guilt, but simply as a bothersome fine to be paid, and in which complex legal activities may keep a known criminal free for many years, will serve to emphasize Nietzsche's point. In primitive, less stable societies, "justice is swift." In the more settled national states of today, it may be unclear, complex, or simply forgotten.

11. True justice, Nietzsche continues, does not grow out of a desire for revenge (rancor), which is a reactive emotion. It grows, rather, out of a the ability to control the reactive emotions of the injured party, by the intervention of an unprejudiced view, which is the province of the powerful or active element in a society. It is the active element that can afford to be just, since its stability is not threatened by offenders. Vengeance, being a reactive emotion, is a sign of dangerous instability, and needs

to be controlled. The very idea of justice, then, is the idea of a control over reactive emotions by means of laws and established arrangements for repayment. According to Nietzsche, the ideas of "right" and "wrong" are entirely dependent upon the establishment of such a legal system. In nature, no act is "right" or "wrong" as such. Only by referring the act to a system of laws can one judge its "rightness" or "wrongness."

Comment

Nietzsche's conception of the dependence of "right" and "wrong" upon a legal system which is primarily designed to secure justice may be contrasted with the ethical system of the English philosopher. John Stuart Mill, for whom "right" and "wrong" were ideas associated with the amount of happiness brought about by a given act. Since the just decision may not always be the one which promotes the most happiness, these two ways of looking at the meaning of "right" and "wrong" are sometimes thought to be irreconcilable. Nietzsche held a very low opinion of Mill. (See J. S. Mill, *Utilitarianism*, especially Chapter Five, "On the Connection between Justice and Utility.")

12-15. Nietzsche returns to the subject of punishment. The origin of punishment must be clearly distinguished from its purpose. It is a mistake to take the purpose of a thing as an explanation of its origin. For example, trees, which may be useful for building shelters, were not "made" for that purpose. To think this way is to "build purposes into nature." If punishment has as its purpose the execution of vengeance, it would still be a mistake to assume that vengeance was the origin of punishment. The search for origins, then, must be governed by historical method, not by a short-cut reference to the present purposes of an institution that is already with us.

Nietzsche distinguishes two aspects of punishment: First, a relatively stable form, the form given it by custom, habit, and law. Second, a relatively changeable function, that is, the purposes to which it is put. He rejects completely the view that punishment arose out of a desire to harm an offender, but insists that this is just one of the many purposes to which punishment may be put. The word "punishment," he says, is really impossible to define in any single way; "only that which has no history can be defined." The best that can be done is to provide a list of some of the many purposes of punishment. Nietzsche gives eleven such purposes, such a inspiring fear, maintaining order, obtaining payment, creating memory, and controlling vengeance.

The view that punishment is of value because it produces a sense of guilt is a mistaken one. Punishment does exactly the opposite. It merely adds to the resistance of the criminal toward guilt feelings. The very acts for which a criminal may be punished are also sometimes carried out by the state itself without guilt, so that guilt and punishment seem unrelated.

Comment

For example, "murder" and "capital punishment." If the state can kill without guilt, why should the murderer feel guilt? Note that the idea of punishment as a repayment for a debt would make it a means of absolving oneself from guilt, rather than a means of producing guilt feelings.

Nietzsche concludes that "bad conscience," which is the feeling of guilt as a discomfort, cannot have originated through the practice of punishment of wrongdoers. What punishment accomplishes, if anything, is the stimulation of a sense of prudence, of avoiding the same mistake again. The philosopher

Spinoza (1632-1677) seems to have reflected this view in looking upon conscience as the simple sadness which accompanies disappointment. Such a conscience, says Nietzsche, is what awakens prudence, but it is not the "bad conscience" in which a man condemns himself as a moral transgressor, and produces feelings of remorse.

16-18. Now Nietzsche states his own view of the origin of "bad conscience." Man, he says, has a tendency to "interiorize"; that is, whenever an instinctive mode of action is blocked, he turns it inward, making himself the sufferer of the action. The "interior world" of man (his soul) thus expands in direct proportion to the degree in which his ability to carry out instinctive behavior is blocked. (In this connection, see *Beyond Good and Evil*, section 257, and the Comment following section 295.) Nietzsche's hypothesis is that the earliest stages of human society were tyrannic, and that the restriction of external freedom by the ruling class led to a seeking of internal freedom, in which the natural desire for conflict, reward, and punishment were turned upon oneself. This, he says, is the germ from which "bad conscience" developed. Since there is a pleasure in the inflicting of cruelty, the individual, in turning inward, inflicts cruelty upon himself. Nietzsche suggests that self-denial, engaged in as a part of this general "program" of self-punishment, is the original source of altruistic values (helping others).

Comment

In this connection, one may refer to *Thus Spoke Zarathustra*. In the discourse *Of Love of One's Neighbor*, Nietzsche introduces the **theme** that love of neighbor is a sign of fear of oneself. "Neighbor-love," as contrasted with "Friendship," is seen as a sign of weakened individuality. The point here is that altruistic values do not derive from utility, but arise merely as a by-product of self-denial, which is a form of self-punishment.

19-21. Nietzsche diverges, momentarily, from his general topic in order to discuss the relation between the notion of guilt and the idea of God. He suggests that ancestor worship grew out of the transference of the creditor-debtor pattern to the relationship between men and their forefathers. As long as the tribe prospers, a continuing "debt" can be felt toward those who made such prosperity possible. Self-punishment, in the form of sacrificial rites, for example, would be one of the few ways in which this debt could be repaid. Nietzsche proposes that the conception of tribal "gods" may have grown out of an increasingly strong regard for the "creditor-ancestors."

Eventually, man looks upon himself as indebted to the gods, and thereby placed under the continual burden of obligation to repay this debt. This sense of the burden of a universal guilt (indebtedness felt as a continuing need for self-punishment) reaches its highest peak in connection with the Christian God, the most powerful God in history. If, as Nietzsche has reason to believe, the belief in God is on the decline, then perhaps there will be a corresponding decline in the sense of universal guilt.

However, the desire for self-punishment is too strong to stop with the idea of God as the eternal creditor. God may be capable of forgiveness, or the debt may be repaid. In order to rule out this possibility, then, nature itself is taken to be guilty, or at least the essential nature of man. There remains, at this point, only the sacrifice of God Himself as a means of paying the debt. In this way, Nietzsche interprets the Christian tradition of the Crucifixion. (*Beyond Good and Evil*, section 55, also deals with this topic.)

22-23. Nietzsche summarizes his view: man's animal nature (especially his desire for the pleasure of cruelty), having been suppressed by the rulers, turns into a need for self-torture. The rationale for such self-inflicted punishment is the feeling of indebtedness, first to ancestors, then to God. Finally, man condemned his own essence, and perhaps even the very structure of all existence, as irredeemably guilty. Nietzsche calls this an "insanity of the will," which is a great sickness in man. He points out, however, that not all gods are constructed in this way. The gods of ancient Greece served an entirely different purpose. These latter gods were blamed for the immoral acts of men, and thus served as a means of ridding oneself of guilt.

24. Nietzsche insists, in concluding, that he is not setting forth an entirely negative doctrine. He realizes that he has dealt harshly with Christianity, but he feels that the "disease" of "bad conscience" requires harsh measures as a cure. The real way out, he states, is a reversal of the association of guilt with natural instincts, and the attaching of guilt to the nihilistic desire for otherworldliness. The strength need for such an upheaval of values, however, is very great, and he foresees that only a "true redeemer," who will reaffirm the value of earthly life, and turn moral condemnation against those who teach man to turn away from himself because he is a creature of eternal guilt, will bring this about. This redeemer, he muses, is precisely his own Zarathustra.

THE GENEALOGY OF MORALS

TEXTUAL ANALYSIS

ESSAY 3

THIRD ESSAY

1-5. The topic of this last essay is the significance of the "ascetic ideals": the ideals of the nonsensual, nonworldly life. Nietzsche introduces the subject with a brief, suggestive account of the reasons for the magnetism which asceticism seems to exert upon artists, philosophers, women, psychopaths, priests, and saints. For each of these, he says, asceticism has a different meaning. For women, it can be no more than an addition to their attractive charms. For the psychopath, it is an excuse for his necessary withdrawal from the world. For priests, it is an instrument of power. This diversity, he suggests, is a sign of an underlying characteristic of the will, a fear of nothingness, of meaninglessness, and a corresponding urge to find meaning, even if meaning can only be found in a denial of life.

In order to clarify his thesis, Nietzsche considers first the case of the composer Richard Wagner, whose opera Parsifal represented a change in attitude toward asceticism, a praise of chastity. Nietzsche sees no real conflict between chastity and sexuality; a good marriage, he says, may "transcend these opposites." The healthy man is capable of a balance between mere animality and austere, intellectual antisensualism. But the ascetic ideal rejects all sensuality. Why did Wagner, as an artist of the highest rank, turn toward this ideal?

Perhaps, Nietzsche admits, he intended the whole thing as an immense joke. Yet Wagner's own behavior, in his later years, did not bear out such an interpretation. The artist, however, must be distinguished from the works of art which he produces. The works themselves are always greater than he is. The artist is merely a catalyst, an inert but necessary factor in the transformation of a deep, irresistible urge into artistic form. As such, the artist senses an isolation from the rest of men, even from reality itself. Wagner's final affiliation with asceticism, then, may have arisen out of a desire to associate himself with a highly respected way of life. He needed "moral support" as his sense of separation from reality increased. To this end, he also accepted the authority of the philosopher Schopenhauer, who placed music in a special "**metaphysical**" category, as an expression of the basic nature of the universe.

6-7. Nietzsche does not find this aspect of the meaning of ascetism to be of much importance. The artist merely seizes upon the ascetic ideal as a means of support. More important is the attachment of a philosopher, like Schopenhauer, to ascetic ideals. Therefore Nietzsche turns his attention to Schopenhauer. That philosopher, he says, adopted the view of his predecessor, Immanuel Kant, that the chief trait of the appreciation of art was an attitude of disinterested contemplation, in which individual desires were absent. For Schopenhauer, this meant that the experience of art constituted a release from the pain of desire-especially from sexual compulsion. Nietzsche does not wholly agree with this view of art, and he interprets Schopenhauer's esteem for art as a means to disinterestedness as a purely personal manifestation of Schopenhauer's own mental state.

Schopenhauer's own esteem for the ascetic ideal (freedom from desire), Nietzsche says, was the result of the fact that he was tormented by desire, and that he found release from this torment in asceticism. In addition, Nietzsche claims that Schopenhauer had an intense need for enemies, a need which was purely a matter of Schopenhauer's own mentality. He found whipping boys ready at hand in "woman" and in "sensuality," and seized upon the ascetic ideal as a rationalization for his enmity.

7-8. Aside from Schopenhauer's own personal psychology, however, there remains a general distaste for sensuality on the part of philosophers. This inclination, Nietzsche believes, is due to the fact that the worldly life leads to responsibilities which inhibit the freedom of the philosopher. Sustained abstract thought is not possible under the pressure of responsibilities of family and business. The ascetic ideal, for philosophers, represents a means of independence. Asceticism gives the philosopher his best working conditions. The three slogans of asceticism are poverty, humility, and chastity; the philosopher's creed is "we are owned by the things we own." Therefore, he avoids ownership in order to be free. He avoids sexual intercourse in order to maintain his strength. He seldom desires children, because he is hopeful of perpetuating himself through his works.

Comment

Nietzsche's account of the place of asceticism in the life of the philosopher is a reasonable one, but only up to a point. It is clear that business and personal involvements are not desirable for one whose calling lies in abstract thought. But this, it may be argued, is only because the philosopher's line of work requires different materials and different "connections" than those required by, for example, the businessman. It is equally true, of course, that the businessman cannot function at his best if his time is interrupted by lengthy intellectual discussions. But the acceptance of certain working conditions does not dictate acceptance of these same conditions as an ideal way of life for all men. The ascetic ideals of poverty and chastity, for example, can function in a detrimental way even for the philosopher; one does not think well on an empty stomach, with bills to pay, and in need of human companionship. Nietzsche's account, up to this point, is disturbingly non-Nietzschean, in that it appears to be under the influence of that old doctrine which he generally detested: the doctrine that mind and body are wholly separate, and its corollary that the mind functions best when totally freed from physical bonds. As if sensing this, Nietzsche continues his account with a somewhat different emphasis.

9-10. At one time, the habits of thought which dominate philosophical technique were contrary to the entire value system of society. Ancient peoples considered irrationality, cruelty, and violent passions as virtues, and madness as a manifestation of the divine. Any cool appraisal, especially if it resulted in a suggestion that some condition or other should be changed, was liable to be viewed with distrust, if not rewarded by death. The philosopher, therefore, had to give himself a special place, and this was accomplished by adopting the ascetic ideal. In this, he allied himself to the religious priesthood, for people were astonished and frightened by men who had the strength to inflict cruelty upon themselves through self-denial. Philosophy, therefore, took on an ascetic disguise. But this stop-gap measure eventually came to be believed in, and the ascetic ideal was wedded to philosophy in a relatively permanent way.

Comment

This view, whether true or false, is a more sophisticated account of the matter. The historical regard for the ascetic ideal on the part of philosophers is seen as a matter of temporary social necessity, not as a permanent need. The mind-body separation, mentioned in the previous Comment, may have sprung from the same necessity: by placing thought in a separate "world' from that of everyday pursuits, a certain degree of protection is obtained. Indeed, in earlier times, it might have been said with truth that the "world" of immediate human commerce simply had no place for abstract intellectual pursuits. A parallel case, perhaps, is the sharp division between "reason" and "faith," as a means of protecting religious beliefs from the attacks of reasoned scepticism. By supposing a realm of "faith," impervious to merely reasoned conclusions, beliefs which cannot stand the test of reason are given a different sanction. (See *Beyond Good and Evil*, section, on the "prejudice of opposites.")

11-14. The ascetic priest, continues Nietzsche, is so attached to the ascetic ideal that this ideal might be said to make up his essence. For this reason, it is foolish to ask the priest to explain the significance of this ideal or to justify it. His own views will be necessarily prejudiced. The ascetic ideal, which condemns life, seems to be universally present in human societies. That such an ideal should flourish is a wonder, for it attacks life itself. The only possible answer is that the ascetic ideal must support life, even while appearing to deny it. This is the paradox of asceticism.

Philosophy, when it denies reality to the world of sense experience, is practicing the ascetic ideal. It reaches a peak of sadism when it affirms the existence of a "true" world, and then places it out of reach. Plato and Kant have both done this. However, this is not entirely bad, because such thought contributes to objectivity by supplying new perspectives. All knowledge, as well as all sense perception, is a matter of perspective. True objectivity lies in the ability to entertain more than one perspective, not in a total absence of perspective.

Nietzsche insists that the paradox of ascetism must be merely an apparent paradox. He believes that the ascetic ideal is a preservative measure which furnishes a meaning for life in a people who have lost all other reason for living. It is the only ideal which will continue to operate in a society which has become weary of life. (See *Beyond Good and Evil*, sections 61-62.)

But such a desperate measure is certainly the reflection of a desperate state of affairs. What is it that renders man sick, that puts him in a position which requires such an extreme remedy?

Comment

Nietzsche has made use of his belief that effects are often mistaken for causes; the ascetic ideal is not a cause of nihilism, but an effect, a symptom, of the underlying disease.

Man's self-pity is partly to blame for this condition. Nietzsche therefore condemns pity, and suggests that a healthy fear of one man by another helps to strengthen individuals. But equally bad, he continues, is a loathing of man. If a large part of mankind is sick, those who are healthy enough to affirm life without qualification must be on guard against extreme pity and loathing. They must not subordinate themselves to the sick by attempting to care for them. The healthy men must be kept apart, even in solitude, if this is necessary, to preserve their integrity.

Comment

This view was exemplified in the story of Zarathustra, who was required to overcome disgust (in *The Convalescent*) and pity (in *The Sign*). Nietzsche's position here regarding the value of mutual fear in promoting strength may be contrasted with his repudiation of fear as a primary human motivation (in *Zarathustra*, part four, Of Science). But Zarathustra's position is not intended for sick men. The value of fear in the present context is only a result of the morbid, or sick, condition of society. In a healthy society, fear would not be of such importance.

15-22. If the healthy man is endangered by becoming an attendant of the sick, those who do attend them must also be sick. These proper attendants are the ascetic priests. They can understand and administer to the sick because they have the same illness.

Comment

The nature of the sickness of which Nietzsche speaks may not seem wholly clear. His meaning seems to shift from physical sickness to psychological sickness. He speaks of nervous disorders (section 15) and of the "born misfit" (section 14). But the apparent confusion is not serious. He is interested in a general psychological state (so general that it might be called a "social" illness), whose earmarks are widespread disillusionment, vindictiveness, explosive emotions, discontent, and superficial moralities; but he holds that the causes of these social weaknesses are, for the most part, physical or physiological. These causes may include the following (section 17): genetic (or racial) weakness resulting from improper breeding; a racial antagonism toward the environment itself (misplaced or migrating populations); widespread acceptance of a poor diet; and general appearance of chronic diseases. Such generalized physiological factors, manifesting themselves as psychological and social weaknesses, constitute the degenerate state of things which raise the ascetic ideals to an important position. The way in which these ideals function as a means of survival is detailed partly in his interpretation of the ascetic priest, which follows. Of special importance, however, is his thesis (in section 15) that the greatest danger to the sick is the presence of the healthy. These, he says, they naturally resent and envy. The priest, then, has to deal with their resentment as well as their illness.

The ascetic priest does not cure; he simply eases pain. He does this in several ways:

1. He gives resentment and envy an outlet, by turning it against a "new object" - the sufferer himself. Since the causes of the sickness are not understood, the sufferer casts about for a responsible party, someone to blame. The priest directs this impulse against the sufferer. He does this by means of the concepts of "guilt," "sin," "perdition," and "damnation" (section 16). The sufferer is made to feel that his discomfort is due to his own guilt, if not for personal evil, then for original sin. Nietzsche, of course, denies that there is any such thing as original sin.

2. He produces a form of hypnosis, in which the pain of existence is easier to bear. This is produced by denying the ego, and by regulating sensual stimulation. Hallucinations and "mystical" religious experiences may result. "Redemption" is an expression of the ultimate in this process of self-negation.

3. He praises mechanical routine in life, as a way of taking the mind of the sufferer off his discomfort (section 18).

4. He promotes the attainment of mild enjoyments, primarily the altruistic ones of charity, comfort, and advice. This includes the promotion of "organization" in the form of charitable groups and the "congregation" (section 18).

5. He also provides for occasional outbursts of intense emotion, such as rage or fear (sections 19-20).

Nietzsche believes that "guilt" and "bad conscience," which he analyzes as a form of self-punishment, are the primary "medications" of the priest. All these things, however, do not simply ease pain; they also make the sick sicker. Widespread epidemics of epilepsy and nervous disorders are the end result of "overdoses" of these "remedies." The ascetic ideal also dulls the sense of beauty. Preference for the New Testament over the Old Testament is a sign of this. The latter is a powerful literary work, the former is artistically poor. (See *Beyond Good and Evil*, section 52.)

23-26. Nietzsche returns to his basic question, that of the meaning of the ascetic ideal itself, and the reason for its wide acceptance. He hints at the answer (but will not state it fully until the last section: 28): it is the expression of a will. Here, he does not clarify this, but points out that the immense power of this system of ideals is the result of its comprehensive scope. It is able to unify, to supply a consistent and widespread interpretation of life for a vast variety of peoples. (Nietzsche has already noted that it also utilizes a deep human instinct and the traits of early social systems - the emotion of revenge, pleasure in cruelty, and the system of reward and punishment.)

The ascetic ideal also flourishes because there are no effective counterforces. One might hope to find a counterideal in intellectual studies, such as science, philosophy, or scholarship. But Nietzsche is disdainful of the scholars of the day. For the most part, scholarship is an empty pursuit. The case is the same for philosophy and science. These are represented by the "unbelievers." The tradition of mistrust and inquiry which guides intellectual activity results in a natural suspicion of the objects of strong belief. Wherever a system of beliefs is supported by a powerful faith, the philosophical spirit finds the likelihood of deception. But those who are so honest that they believe in nothing at all are possessed by the most subtle and strongest aspect of the ascetic ideal, the belief in absolute truth. Knowledge is really a matter of viewpoint, and the desire for absolute truth leads to a denial of the world as it is, because the immediate qualities of things about us are highly affected by the values and viewpoints from which we approach them. The belief in "objectivity," then, simply leads to a denial of the world of values, and is, as such, another manifestation of the ascetic ideal.

Nietzsche recalls his earlier point: that inquiry and philosophy, historically speaking, had to ally themselves with the ascetic way of life (section 9). Art is closer to being a counter-influence, for the reason that illusion or the lie, as well as stimulation of the senses, are present in it. But even artists can be corrupted. (See *Zarathustra*, part four, The Sorcerer.) Even Immanuel Kant's view that questions of a theological nature were not knowable by means of reason was not sufficient to counteract the ascetic ideal and the will to absolute truth. Finally, Nietzsche rejects the possibility that historians can provide an antidote. Their emphasis upon "pure" description is taken to be another sign of the will to truth.

27. Nietzsche points out that he intends to discuss the historical effects of the ascetic ideal in a future book (*The Will to Power*). His main point here is to insist that the ascetic ideal is not counteracted by rigorous intellectuality, even by atheism, but is in fact reinforced by these. Christian ethics have raised truthfulness to a high position, and now this desire for truth is about to destroy the ethical system itself. Atheism and scientific scepticism regarding moral values are not at odds with this primary value of Christianity, the value of truth. And since asceticism and the will to truth go hand in hand, atheism and science are not really contrary to the ascetic ideal.

28. What, then, does the ascetic ideal signify? It represents the only way in which man can give meaning to his will-at least, the only way he has found so far, for this is the greatest problem he has to face. Before the ascetic ideal arose, man, could find no meaning at all for his existence, and therefore all expressions of will were essentially futile. In addition, man suffers from a variety of illnesses. He was unable to give meaning either to his will or to his suffering. But the ascetic ideal, which makes the denial of life into the very meaning of life, gives both will and suffering a meaning. It is able to sustain itself, because it draws for support upon the very same meaninglessness and suffering which it alleviates. It is, all the same, a will to nothingness. But, Nietzsche concludes, man would rather have nothingness for his purpose, than have no purpose at all.

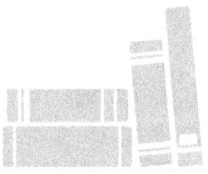

INTRODUCTION TO THUS SPOKE ZARATHUSTRA

Nietzsche's *Thus Spoke Zarathustra* was written in the period 1883-1885. The name "Zarathustra" derives from the Persian "Zoroaster." Zoroaster was the founder of ancient Persia's national faith which included the doctrine that there was a continual struggle in the cosmos between a good and evil deity. Nietzsche's philosophy, however is not to be identified with that faith.

Because of its poetic style and its wealth of literary values, many have found it difficult to approach as a work of philosophy. The English composer Frederick Delius (1862-1934) used portions of the text in his extensive choral work. A Mass of Life. In this book, which is generally thought to be his greatest work, Nietzsche puts forth the three conceptions that are most closely associated with his philosophy: the Superman, the Will to Power, and Eternal Recurrence. These three ideas are the center of his attempt to deal with the problem of finding a basis from which one may build new values in a world where the old foundation of values-religion-was, as he saw it, falling down on every side under the influence of science. This loss of a supernatural basis for values he expressed by the phrase, "God is dead."

The book is divided into four parts. The first three part form a unit, in which part two is both an elaboration of the ideas in the first part, and a transition to the third part. The fourth section was originally meant to be the beginning of a second trilogy, which was never completed.

THUS SPOKE ZARATHUSTRA

TEXTUAL ANALYSIS

PART 1

| Zarathustra's Prologue

At the age of thirty, Zarathustra leaves his home to seek solitude in a mountain retreat. There he lives for ten years, accompanied by his eagle and his serpent (his pride and his wisdom), until he comes to feel that he is overflowing with wisdom. He likens himself to the sun, which overflows with light and warmth, and he asks the sun, "What would be your happiness, if you had not those for whom you shine!" He decides to communicate his wisdom to others, and resolves to descend from the mountain. This is called "Zarathustra's down-going" and may mean his destruction as well as his descent.

On his way, he meets an old man, who notes that Zarathustra now appears to be clear-eyed, free from disgust, light of step, and innocent, like an awakened child. The old hermit, seeing that Zarathustra intends to distribute his wisdom among mankind, warns him that he may be received badly. But Zarathustra laughs, and proceeds on his way, saying: "Could it be possible! This old saint has not yet heard in his forest that God is dead!"

Arriving at the nearest town, Zarathustra speaks to a multitude of people gathered in the market place, where they have assembled to watch a tightrope walker, He tells them that there is something beyond man, and that man must be overcome, in order to reach the beyond-man, the "Superman." The Superman, he says, is the "meaning of the earth," and he warns them to reject those who place faith in nonearthly hopes.

Zarathustra tells them that the greatest experience is to reject happiness, reason, virtue, justice, or pity as justification for existence. He praises only the man who looks upon himself as a bridge to something better, and who therefore, in a way, looks for his own destruction. The most contemptible man, in contrast, is the "ultimate man," who tries to fix all things in their places, and to preserve himself at all costs. Such a man shuns all risk, he is static and unmoving, and he fears chaos above all else. But chaos is a condition of creativity, says Zarathustra - "one must have chaos in one, to give birth to a dancing star."

The people, however, do not understand him. Just then, the tightrope walker, who is on his way across the rope over the heads of the crowd, is unbalanced by a buffoon, and falls to the ground. The acrobat, dying from the injuries of his fall, expresses his fear that the Devil is dragging him to Hell. But Zarathustra says, "There is no Devil and no Hell." Upon hearing this, the man is seized by the unhappy thought that if there is no afterlife, his own life on earth has been no better than that of an animal. "Not so," says Zarathustra, explaining that the man had risked destruction through his own calling, and that this is a noble thing. Zarathustra promises to bury the man with his own hands.

Zarathustra sits with the dead man until dark, whereupon he raises the body to his back, and begins to walk to a burial place. On the way, the buffoon and then a band of grave diggers deride him and warm him to stay away from the town. As he proceeds into the woods, Zarathustra becomes hungry. He receives food at the house of a hermit, and then continues to a point at which the road ends, where he buries the body of the acrobat in a hollow tree. Then he falls asleep.

When he awakens, it is already noon, and Zarathustra has come to understand a "new truth." He resolves to seek companions who will assist him in the destruction of old values and the creation of new ones. Henceforth, then, he will not speak to the masses, who have rejected him, but to a select few who can understand and aid him in the harvesting of wisdom. Just as the sun does not shine upon those who cannot feel its warmth, Zarathustra cannot give his wisdom to those who will not understand. Therefore he sets out to find these creative companions.

Comment

The tightrope walker represents man, suspended over the abyss between his present state and the Superman. The buffoon is "ultimate man," who fears the creative journey, and who therefore fears the creative man, in whom he sees only chaos and madness. (Zarathustra's comment that creativity demands an element of chaos is clearly related to Nietzsche's earlier view, in *The Birth of Tragedy*, that true art must spring from Dionysian formlessness.) Zarathustra is impressed by the resistance of the ideals of the crowd, represented by "ultimate man." They have both rejected him and destroyed the fearless rope walker, who, in seeking his own downfall, shows qualities admired by Zarathustra. The doctrine of the earthly Superman, as the final goal of a mankind freed of supernatural hopes, is here linked to the overcoming of one's own ego. Nietzsche develops this **theme** in the next section.

ZARATHUSTRA'S DISCOURSES

Of The Three Metamorphoses

The spirit of one who would become a companion of Zarathustra, and thus a philosopher, the bridge to the Superman, must undergo three changes. First, it must bear the weight of humility, refuse to complain of hardship, seek the truth above all else, and submit to searching self-criticism. At this stage, the spirit is likened to a camel, the beast of burden. Second, it must reject all systems of values which are externally imposed. It must answer the command "thou shalt!" with a "sacred No"; this is the spirit of the lion, and represents freedom to create new values. Third, it must make a new beginning out of "innocence and forgetfulness," and this is the spirit of the child. Only in this condition may the spirit create new worlds of value. It is the child-spirit that affirms a new existence, a "sacred Yes."

Of The Chairs Of Virtue

Zarathustra comes across a "wise man" who teaches young men to be virtuous in all things, so that they may sleep well at night, and suffer no discomfort from nagging conscience or disturbing thoughts of nonconformity. They should honor authority (even if it is dishonest), make peace with man and God, and turn away from honor and wealth. Sleep is called "the lord of virtues." Zarathustra calls these "opium virtues," and says that such a doctrine would be useful only if life had no sense at all.

Of The Afterworldsmen

Next Zarathustra condemns those who would seek salvation in a world beyond this one. He says that all Gods are human creations, and that the "other world" is a "heavenly nothing." He, himself, once thought of the world as the joyful image of an other world reality which was without form or image - the "imperfect image of contradiction." But even this view, he says, was a false hope, a mere construction of his sown mind. The only true reality is the human ego, or self, which is the measure of all things. This ego is earthly; it is a part of the body, and it alone can create meaning for the earth. Zarathustra urges mankind to turn away from the desire for "afterworlds" and to find "a new will" which desires the earthly path and values it highly.

Of The Despisers Of The Body

Zarathustra has a message for those who despise the body (even as the afterworldsman may despise the earth in his zeal to reach beyond it). He teaches that intelligence, the spirit, and the soul are instruments of the body. The true "self" is not the soul- which is but an instrument-but is the organism which behaves both spiritually and intelligently; that is, an organism which values and which thinks. The body, he says, does not say "I," but performs "I."

Thus there is a Self which lies behind the spirit. Those who seek to create worlds beyond the body and the earth are not only doomed to disappointment; they bring the self to seek its own destruction by demanding the impossible. Thus they become despisers of the true Self, the body, without knowing the source of their distaste. Zarathustra rejects such men. They are not the creators he seeks.

Comment

In these last three sections, Zarathustra attacks that form of pessimism which Nietzsche called nihilism. Those who support the public standard of values - a standard imposed from without, rather than springing from within - and those who find the foundation for virtues in a nonearthly realm, are condemned, because the unquestioning belief in such standards, according to Nietzsche, leads to sickness and self-destruction (with no prospect of self-renewal). This happens because such standards cannot be maintained, but all value has been based upon their being maintained. These men (who are in the class of the "ultimate man" discussed in the Prologue) are now seen to be the opposite of the creative ones discussed in Of the Three Metamorphoses. These latter have gained their freedom from the "dragon" of standard values and recognize the biological truth that even man's spiritual and intellectual side are but parts of his earthly evolution. It should be noted that the passage in Of the Afterworldsmen, in which Zarathustra repudiates his own earlier belief in an otherworldly reality, has been taken as Nietzsche's own rejection of his doctrine in *The Birth of Tragedy* that the justification for life is art.

Of Joys And Passions

The man who finds the source of virtue within himself, prepares thereby for the step of overcoming himself (which will lead to the child-state of the true creator). Such a man does not deny the passions, but affirms them, and is able to find values of which the very passions themselves are the source. Thus his passions become his joys. Conflict among virtues is a necessary thing, and no external doctrine can unify them, but only a unity of the Self.

Comment

Here Zarathustra shows us the opposite of the despisers of the body, in whom passion is something to be subdued by virtue, and is in conflict with virtue. He is describing the "spirit of the lion" in Of The Three Metamorphoses, in which the "thou shalt" becomes "I Will"; that is, the Self, not an external standard, becomes the source of value.

Of The Pale Criminal

Turning from the psychology of virtue to the psychology of crime, Zarathustra speaks to the judges of a murderer. He says that the man is not to be condemned for being immoral (for violating a moral code). If this were so, even the judges may be condemned, because all have committed crimes in thought. Thought, however, does not cause action, and the cause of this man's act was not criminal thought or motive, in which all may share, but rather disease. Morality itself is a relative thing - "there have been other ages and another evil and good" - and cannot serve as a basis for punishment. Punish the criminal, rather, as an enemy, an invalid, or a fool, but not as a sinner. The judges attempt to interpret the murder as an immoral act, prompted by the motive of theft. But Nietzsche interprets the theft as a rationalization, an excuse, which the criminal required in order to avoid admitting to himself the real truth - that he desired, in madness, to commit murder. Such a criminal is sick, and if we treat him merely as a healthy man who has developed "bad" motives, we have misunderstood the nature of the criminal mind.

Comment

This is an advanced and important view of crime, which is consistent with Nietzche's view that the foundation for virtue is not in externally imposed standards, but within the self. For if morality springs from individuals, how are questions of moral responsibility for criminal acts to be answered? How can anyone be held responsible or punished for a crime, if each man is a source of his own moral rules? Against this charge that his view leads to anarchy (each man for himself), Nietzsche proposes a complete upset of the traditional ground for the condemnation of criminals, and suggests instead a naturalistic ground: they are punishable as enemies and fools, but also treatable as are the diseased and invalids. The causes of crime are not moral infirmities, but psychological and social defects. Hence the question of the treatment of criminals is outside the moral sphere entirely, and Nietzsche's doctrine that each man creates his own virtue does not lead to a condonation of criminality.

Of Reading And Writing

Nietzsche, through the voice of Zarathustra, speaks of his own method of writing-his "aphoristic" style, made up of short, often difficult, passages. The depth of meaning to be found in personal insight cannot be expressed clearly in common terms, for the very reason that the common terms represent what is common to all, and what he wishes to express is often something personal and quite uncommon. Therefore he expresses himself in aphorisms, which part of the reader, which plodding intellect and fixed patterns of thought cannot match. To understand the very heart of the writer requires a rejection of "the spirit of gravity" which pulls one down by the weight of familiar patterns, and a free sensitivity to that personal communication which cannot be accomplished by the common forms of language. Therefore Zarathustra admonishes, "Write with blood ... He who are like mountain peaks: reaching them requires a leap on the writes in blood and aphorisms does not want to be read, he wants to be learned by heart."

Comment

Compare Nietzsche's view here with his view of limitations of language, expressed in *The Birth of Tragedy* (see the sections above titled The Spirit of Music and Positive Influence of Socrates).

Of The Tree On The Mountainside

Zarathustra speaks to a youth who is unhappy because, in trying to elevate his soul after the example of Zarathustra, he finds himself becoming more and more contemptuous of himself. Zarathustra points to the tree beside which they stand, and likens the youth's quest to the growth of the tree. As the tree grows higher, it also puts out deeper roots. But deep in the soul are passions and evils which have long been denied and condemned by the seeker of wisdom. The higher the tree grows, the nearer it comes to its own destruction-by lightning. In the same way the youth, in seeking wisdom, also approaches his own destruction. But this is the necessary step on the road to wisdom. The noble man holds true to his course. His baser instincts must be brought out into the open-he must come fearlessly to self-knowledge before he can "overcome himself," and truly create new values. Zarathustra contrasts the noble man and the "good" man. The noble man desires to bring forth new things; the "good" man wants to preserve the old. (Thus they are related as the Superman to the "ultimate man".) There are noble men who have failed in the attempt to reach self-knowledge, but have retreated into a world of sensual pleasures. Zarathustra rejects these men as much as he rejects the "good" man. (The realization that the spirit is an instrument of the body does not mean that attention to bodily pleasures are to be made supreme. To do so is to misunderstand the nature of the body.)

Of The Preachers Of Death

Zarathustra renews his attack on nihilism. For those who have already placed the highest values in an unreachable, otherworldly realm, the only choices left for life on earth are "lusts" or "self-mortification." Since lusts are considered bad (and Nietzsche agrees that sensuality, by itself, is an evil), the only course left is self-mortification, which is a turning away from life. This line of thought leads eventually to the dictum: "life itself is suffering." Zarathustra, however, condemns this point of view.

Comment

Nietzsche appears to be criticizing certain aspects of Buddhism, as well as nihilism. The first element of Buddha's "fourfold truth" is that life is pain.

Of War And Warriors

Zarathustra praises "warriors" in this much misunderstood passage. The true warrior hates his enemy, but he does not despise him, for his enemy reflects his own love of bravery. The warrior must rise above shame regarding hatred, envy, and ugliness. Obedience (to a rule) is necessary for the "warrior." He is not a bridge to the Superman, because to him the "thou shalt" is more important than "I will." He obeys rather than creates. But he has the virtues of bravery, pride, and steadfastness in his calling (virtues similar to those observed in the rope walker in the Prologue).

Comment

This passage may be contrasted with the one titled Of the Chairs of Virtue. Nietzsche here opposes the "wise" man's doctrine that virtue is a means to sleep, with the doctrine that peace is to be loved only as "a means to new wars." But the conflict he refers to as "war" is a conflict of ideas, not weapons. The obedience he speaks of may then be obedience to the rules of logic and of science, which, as we saw in *The Birth of Tragedy*, he does not believe to be the ultimate answer to the riddles of life. (Regarding "obedience," see also *Beyond Good and Evil*, aphorism 188.)

Of The New Idol

Zarathustra criticizes "the State," which he contrasts with "peoples" and "herds." A people has its own morality, which is custom and law. Custom and law, in turn, grow from within, from natural conditions of the association of the people. The State puts a superficial unity upon peoples, imposing an external standard of good and evil. But loyalty to such a standard is idol worship, and the State is a false idol. The mark of such a false standard is the emergence of a confusion of good and evil, because the State pretends to reconcile real differences which cannot truly be reconciled from without. The State seeks to attract noble men to its cause, because the loyalty of noble men gives the appearance of nobility to the State. In the modern State, the creative works of men are turned to bad ends (for example, the use of great inventions for purposes of warfare). The public media of communication, such as newspapers, do nothing to improve the people, but instead simply reinforce the false ideals of the State. The State also stimulates the desire for money, catering to the desire for power on the part of weak persons. Zarathustra urges "great souls" to leave the state and to seek solitude.

Of The Flies Of The Market Place

Again Zarathustra tells the truly creative men to turn their backs on the great mass of men. This time, however, it is a warning. The obedient masses, by their sheer numbers, are capable of destroying the great man, in the same way that the slow erosion of rain and root may eventually destroy even massive monuments. The masses may pretend to praise creative men, but they are treacherous, because they sense that creative men are also destroyers of values. Their true loyalty lies with "the actor," a man who is inflexible, who depends upon common "proof" for all things, and who denies the truths which come only to the select few as a result of their self-knowledge (refer to Of Reading and Writing).

Comment

The last two passages repeat Zarathustra's desire to turn away from the populace and to seek the companionship of fellow thinkers. In the first, Of the New Idol, Nietzsche introduces the notion that the source of moral codes may be traced to some natural condition of true community, as opposed to the State. This idea is one which he develops in his later work, *The Genealogy of Morals*. The "actor" in Of The Flies of the Market Place may be the "ultimate man" referred to in the Prologue, but he also appears to have the characteristics of the scientist, the religious leader, and perhaps even the politician, all of whom may represent support for the idol of the State.

Of Chastity; Of The Friend

In these two discourses, Zarathustra compares two kinds of human relationships: the love between man and woman, and the love of friend for friend. Woman, he says, is both a slave and a tyrant. She is blind to everything that she cannot love, and therefore asks too much of her lover; she asks him to be what she wants, not what he is. She commands him through the power of lust. Thus she is, indeed, a slave and a tyrant, but never a friend. Friends, however, stand in a different relationship. To be a true friend, one must respect those things in the other which may even be harmful to oneself. Friends preserve and lead one another, because each sees himself in the other. For Zarathustra, true companionship must be friendship.

Of The Thousand And One Goals

In this important passage, Nietzsche introduces two conceptions which have been only hinted at in the earlier discourses. The first is that morality is a natural development in the life of social groups. The second is his famous principle of the "will to power."

Zarathustra states that he has seen many people, and as many moral codes as there are people. Moral codes are the result of evaluating, and evaluating is instrumental; that is, for the purpose of maintaining and promoting the health of the society. Hence the moral code of a people is determined by the common need, as well as the common environment. The values of a people are called its "overcomings." The values which a group has express its will to power. If these values serve the group well, it will flourish and gain in power. Zarathustra compares the Greeks, the Persians, the Jews, and the Germans, and points out that they all valued that which led them to greatness. These values or moral precepts included such differing rules as "love no one, except your friend," "speak the truth," "honor father and mother," and "practice loyalty ... even in evil and dangerous causes."

Men create values, and the process of evaluation is true creativity. Values themselves are subordinate to the creative process of evaluation. It is the process alone, the means and not the end, that is most important. Originally, values were the exclusive concern of "peoples." The creation of values by individuals in a later development. Even the individual himself is a late development in the history of man. A certain bravery is a condition of creation, since all creation involves a degree of destruction. The presence of a value system, therefore, is a sign of the presence of power. But as long as there are many goals and values, there will be many peoples. Only when there is one goal for all, will there be one "humanity."

Comment

Nietzsche's view that morality is a development for the sake of power may be called moral naturalism and instrumentalism. In this discourse, he brings together many elements from previous parts of the book. His view that the spirit-intellect is instrumental to the well-being of the self, expressed in Of the Despisers of the Body, is not only a correlated idea, but it is suggestive of a later development: that the spirit-intellect (Geist in German) may have an important role to play in the creation of values. His instrumentalism, however, differs from the view of the British philosopher John Stuart Mill, which is sometimes referred to by the same term. For Mill, moral values were instruments for the production of happiness. For Nietzsche, moral values are "overcomings" which do not necessarily lead to happiness, but to power.

What Nietzsche means by "overcoming" is obviously very important. From the first, Zarathustra has said that "Man is something that should be overcome." This is a **metaphor**, and does not mean that man is literally to be destroyed.

In The Tree on the Mountainside, the youth who aspires to be a noble man finds that the nearer he comes to this goal, the more he fears that he will destroy himself. He feels a growing contempt for himself that he cannot understand. Zarathustra replies that his "bad instincts" are seeking to become free. Here he hints at the meaning of "overcoming." The noble man must free all of his nature, what has been thought good and what has been thought evil. The evils (the "fierce dogs") must not be repressed or denied - they must, instead, be given a new form which is not destructive. This process of allowing a destructive instinct to express itself in a nondestructive form has been called "sublimation" (a psychological concept associated with the German psychologist Sigmund Freud). For example, sexual desires may become sublimated in the form of love, or in artistic endeavor. There is a similarity between this process of sublimation and the idea of the imposition of Apollonian form upon Dionysian chaotic forces that was the subject matter of *The Birth of Tragedy*.

But Nietzsche says in the present passage that values are "overcomings." He appears, therefore, to link the psychological concept to the concept of valuation. In order to understand this, it is necessary to note the connection between values and rules or standards of conduct. When a rule is made and followed, it presupposes a value (for example, the rules that govern good driving are "aimed" at the values of safety and the unimpeded progress of traffic). Any new value, or goal, will express itself in the form of new rules and standards, both for individuals and for groups. Thus the form which a sublimated instinct takes represents in fact a valuation. We may correlate this process with the stage of spiritual development given in Of the Three Metamorphoses. First, there is the self-criticism which eventually destroys old rules and standards (the spirit of the camel). This destruction, however, releases tendencies and desires which were previously held in check by the old rules. This new freedom is represented by the spirit of the lion. It is, however, nondirectional, it has no form or aim. There follows an "overcoming," which consists in the formulating of new values and their related rules, in which the newly released tendencies are "sublimated" by being given a new and nondestructive form (the spirit of the child). Sublimation and valuation are related, then, in that the form which the sublimation takes is a direct expression of a value or goal.

Of Love Of One's Neighbor

Here Nietzsche elaborates upon his idea that the true individual is a late comer to the historical scene. Zarathustra says that the "You" is older than the "I," and he chides those who love their neighbors, as people who are really afraid of themselves. He says, "I teach you not the neighbor but the friend." He urges the would-be noble man to seek the man of the future, instead of the "neighbor."

Comment

The implication here is that so long as one's identity is still dependent upon the group, one cannot overcome himself. Yet he is not denying the value of human companionship. He is contrasting "neighbor-love" with "friendship," even as he previously contrasted "woman's-love" with "friendship." The better human relations must promote individuality, and neither wound it nor dull it.

The Way Of The Creator

Abandoning the group, or the "herd," as Zarathustra calls it, is the "way to yourself." It is a hard way, because the herd calls it a crime to seek loneliness. This valuation will still weigh upon the conscience of the lonely one. True freedom, indeed, is not just freedom from the herd. It is freedom to create new values. It is not easy to do this alone, to suffer in the knowledge that only you are responsible for your creation. At the crucial moment, the specter of nihilism (the conviction that "all is false") will raise its voice. This is the necessary consequence of the self-criticism that the noble man must undertake. Zarathustra says: "You must be ready to burn yourself in your own flame: how could you become new, if you had not first become ashes?"

Comment

This recalls clearly the discourse Of the Three Metamorphoses. Most of the preceding discourses may now be seen as an elaboration of this **theme**, with the "new truth" which came to Zarathustra at the conclusion of the Prologue as the real starting point. The true **theme** is the relation of the individual to the group, and the development of real individuality.

Of Old And Young Women

An old woman asks Zarathustra to give her his opinion of Women. He replies: Woman's goal is pregnancy. For Woman, Man is a means, and also a child. Woman is therefore a danger to Man, for she looks upon him as a means to her fulfillment. Man, however, desires danger, and for him, Woman is "the most dangerous plaything." He must always maintain his own will, or Woman will divert him to her purposes. The old woman, to whom Zarathustra is speaking, then imparts her own wisdom: when visiting among woman, always remember to carry a whip. Zarathustra is grateful, and looks upon her words as "a little truth."

Of The Adder's Bite

Zarathustra tells the following story: while he was sleeping, an adder bit him on the neck. Aroused from sleep, he thanked the adder for having awakened him, and behaved as if the poison would do no harm. The snake responded by licking the wound. When Zarathustra's disciples ask him the meaning of his story, he speaks to them of Justice, and the treatment of the wrongdoer. Do not shame your enemy, he says, but show him instead that he has done you a good turn. Take revenge if you wish, but treat the revenge as "an honor" for the guilty one. He condemns "cold justice" that directs itself only to the punishment of the offender, ignoring the guilt of the judges themselves.

Comment

We may recall that in the discourse Of The Pale Criminal, Zarathustra contrasted treating the criminal as an enemy (which he endorses) with treating him as a sinner (which he condemns). He has even spoken of friends as enemies, in the discourse Of the Friend. This doctrine, which seems to make friends of enemies and enemies of friends, is not as strange as it may appear. Zarathustra is condemning the Christian doctrine of "turning the other cheek," blessing your enemy in order to shame him, because this amounts to condemning him as a sinner. The enemy's value is that he reveals weaknesses (as well as strengths) in oneself, as Zarathustra indicated when he thanked the adder for having "awakened" him. He may, in fact, bring us to a knowledge of our own guilt, and thereby to a new "overcoming." Therefore his teaching is: If you are struck by an enemy, search yourself for the way in which you have benefited. If a friend is one who does you good, then an enemy is already half a friend, and a friend is a mirror of yourself. In a broader sense, Zarathustra is opposing the way of seeing things which divides the world into "good guys" and "bad guys" - the "righteous" and the "sinners." He is advocating a new moral view, one that recognizes the mutual responsibility for crime.

Of Marriage And Children

Zarathustra asks of the would-be husband and father: should you desire a child? Only the man who has overcome himself deserves to raise children. True marriage is defined by a common goal: to create a child that is more than its parents. This goal is both the meaning and the truth of marriage. A bad marriage is a terrible thing, causing the child to suffer. The man who has not overcome himself becomes a mere woman's servant, and begets a weeping child. The will to marriage should, instead, be "a longing for the Superman."

Comment

Opponents of Nietzsche may look upon this passage as an affirmation of the "racism" and "genetic selection" doctrine associated with the Nazis. This, however, would be a mistake. The idea of the Superman is neither evolutionary (in the biological sense) nor racial; it is a psychological notion, and it applies to all men. Far from being an immoralist who subordinates the sacred institution of marriage to biological selection, Nietzsche sanctifies marriage, by insisting that the begetting of children creates a great and sacred responsibility. What he teaches is this: if the parent has created a bad child, let him look into himself for the causes. If one would become the parent of a good child, let him first overcome himself. To feel Nietzsche's point more fully, one need only look to the attention being given in modern times to the role of family life in the creation of neuroses, juvenile delinquency, and then, perhaps, a new generation of bad parents. If this circle is to be broken, says Nietzsche, Man must take a new look at himself and his relationships with others.

Of Voluntary Death

A noble man, Zarathustra says, should "die at the right time." Death is important, a cause for celebration, a time for festivities, because it is capable of being a consummation and a promise of hope to the living. This, he says, is the best sort of death. Death should not be your master, but should come as you wish it. The time for desiring death is the time which most benefits one's goals and heirs. Death becomes, then, the passing on of a goal to those who follow after.

Comment

This passage has at least two interpretations. Nietzsche attacks the Christian idea of death as a transition to an afterworld. He faces the question, "How can life be made worthwhile, if death is final and complete destruction?" We may recall Zarathustra's reassurance to the tightrope walker, in the prologue: that his death was not meaningless, because he had perished through his own calling. This suggests that if death is final, we should turn our attention to life and live well. Then, at least, death will not catch us with regrets.

We may also take this passage in a metaphorical sense: "death" may refer to the process of self-overcoming, which may, perhaps, be repeated whenever a goal is reached or a position of stability achieved. Nietzsche has used the **metaphor** of death and rebirth before, for example, in the discourse Of the Way of the Creator. He speaks of overcoming as self-destruction, and of creativity as the result of "a new beginning" (the spirit of the child).

In both cases, a view of goals is implied. Goals, Nietzsche appears to be saying, are not the end (conclusion) of action. They are turning points, the time for a fresh start. This is contrary to a view of life which sees the supreme goal of Man in the attainment of a stable condition, which is so complete that no more effort or action is necessary. Life, for Nietzsche, is action, and since all action is subject to danger, life is as dangerous as it may be rewarding. In a truly rich life, there must be many "deaths," many down-goings, many overcomings. The "ultimate man," with his fear of the unsettled, is the truly dead one. For the Superman, the reaching of one goal is the sign to move on to the next. This sheds some light, perhaps, upon a passage in Of the Three Metamorphoses, in which Zarathustra suggests that one should desert one's cause even "when it is celebrating its victory."

The Bestowing Virtue

Zarathustra, feeling again the need to be alone, prepares to leave his disciples. They present him with a golden staff, upon which is the image of a sun in the coils of a serpent. Regarding this symbol, Zarathustra begins a discussion of virtue. There are, he says, two kinds of selfishness. One is a virtue, the other is a sign of degeneracy. Virtuous selfishness is a selfishness in which the soul seeks to increase its own richness only in order to bestow the fruits of this richness upon others. This is the "bestowing virtue," and its symbol is the sun. One who possesses such a virtue bestows as the sun does, because it cannot help itself. The second kind of selfishness consists in mere taking without giving, and it is a sign of degeneracy.

The serpent around the sun is a symbol of knowledge. Knowledge is a guide and companion to virtue, and the mind of the virtuous man serves to provide him with ideals, to which he must aspire. Blessed in his capacity as a creator and a giver, his body is elevated, his heart is full, and he is at peace with himself. Zarathustra continues by encouraging his disciples to place their loyalty in the earth, and in the "human meaning" of the earth. He again likens man to an evolving animal, and expresses his hope that the evolution of man will give him a victory of meaning over meaninglessness. He repeats his doctrine that the Superman must create just such earthly values. He reminds them, however, of the importance of self-overcoming in this task: the one who would heal others must first heal himself.

Finally, Zarathustra instructs his disciples to turn their critical abilities even upon their leader. He says that the aim of a teacher is not to create pupils, but to create new teachers. He will return to them therefore, only after they have asserted their own individualities and have denied him. He predicts that he will leave and return to them yet a third time, when humanity stands at the midpoint of its development toward the Superman. This moment he calls the "great Noontide." The first part closes with a restatement of the message of the Prologue: God is dead; the new meaning of all things is to be the Superman.

Comment

This is one of the most beautifully composed discourses in the book. It is largely a recapitulation, a return to the beginning material. Zarathustra's discussion of the bestowing virtue is given in terms of the same image to which he likened himself in the Prologue: the sun. And the serpent, which he called his wisdom in the Prologue, is here again present as a symbol of knowledge.

We may note that the Greek god Apollo is associated with the sun. There are other indications that Nietzsche had Apollo in mind, in using the sun as the symbol of the bestowing virtue. In the present discourse, Zarathustra says, "Whenever your spirit wants to speak in images, pay heed; for that is when your virtue has its origins and beginnings." Apollo, we may recall, is the god of image-making (see *The Birth of Tragedy*). There is a similarity between the Apolloian conquest of the Dionysian, in which form is imposed upon the chaotic creative urge of Dionysos, and the idea of sublimation or "overcoming" (see the Comment following the passage Of the Thousand and One Goals). Even the usual example of sublimation, that of sexual desire channeled into other activities, is present in Nietzsche's conception of the Dionysian, which he likened to primitive springtime revelry and "sexual licentiousness." But even if sublimation is similar to Apollonian control over Dionysian urges, the context is different: in the earlier work, it was artistic value which resulted. Here, it is moral value, as the word "virtue" implies. Similarly, the "fierce dogs" of the hidden passions, which can be compared with the Dionysian destructive forces, are not taken by Nietzsche to be representative of some deeper "reality," as was the Dionysian element. Finally, it may be noted that the serpent, wisdom, which might be taken to represent the Socrates of *The Birth of Tragedy*, has here become an ally and companion of Apollo (the sun), and not his enemy. It is not wise, perhaps, to attempt to "carry over" the concepts of the earlier book, unchanged, into the present work. Yet it is also clear that *The Birth of Tragedy* has not been wholly forgotten by its author.

Nietzsche's naturalism is also evident in his interpretation of the "bestowing virtue" as a natural overflow of benefit to others. It is a natural "bestowing" that results from a harmony of body and mind, rather than one which results from a domination and overpowering of the body of the spirit.

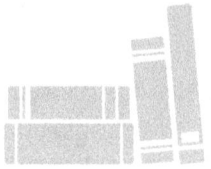

THUS SPOKE ZARATHUSTRA

TEXTUAL ANALYSIS

PART 2

The Child With The Mirror

Zarathustra returns to his mountain solitude, where he remains for several years, while his wisdom grows. At length he is stirred by a dream, in which a child shows him a mirror, and in this mirror his own reflection is replaced by a grinning devil. Zarathustra, interprets this dream as a sign that his teachings have been distorted by his enemies. He resolves to return to his disciples, who are dwelling in the "blessed isles."

Zarathustra is convinced that a change has taken place within his own soul. He is possessed by a happiness that has grown out of loneliness and grief. He is ready now to strike out in a new direction, to speak in new ways. His happiness and his love are so great that they are painful to him, and he is concerned that his message will be too strongly put, so that it may frighten his disciples because of its strength. He does not expect to speak to them softly, as a shepherd plays his flute, but rather to speak with the voice of the storm.

Comment

Even though this passage is similar to the Prologue, there are some subtle changes. In the earlier section, Zarathustra was "weary" and desired the happiness which could be supplied by contact with his fellow men. Like a child, he was innocent, and proceeded with his "down-going" over the warnings of the hermit in the wood. In the present discourse, Zarathustra entertains no illusions. He now knows his friends and his enemies, and he has found new ways to deliver his message. Now he speaks of wisdom as a "lioness," calling to mind the affirmative spirit of the lion, in Of the Three Metamorphoses. This may be an indication that the first three parts of the book are intended to reflect Zarathustra's own passing through the three stages of the soul (the camel, the lion, and the child).

Of The Blissful Isles

Zarathustra begins with an expansion of the **theme** that opened and closed part one, the idea that God is dead. God is a "supposition," and it is wrong to suppose that the ideal goals of man should rest in something which cannot be understood or attained. Only in goals that are within human limitations, can man find a hope which will sustain him. Zarathustra teaches that the goal of man should remain bounded by what is thinkable by man. Therefore, he denies that there are Gods. It is evil, he says, to teach the existence of something that is wholly perfect, unmoved, and unchanging. This can lead to a rejection of the changing world in which we all must live. We should, instead, reject the conception of an entirely stable world, in which there are fixed values, and praise this changing world, because change permits creation. It is creation which gives value to life, and creation requires the greatest of changes: dying, renewal, and the pain of birth. We should, in consequence, also value will, because willing frees us from fixed patterns and is the starting point of the creative process. Will, evaluation, creation, and knowledge are the values which are most important in a changing world.

Zarathustra likens the Superman of the future to "an image sleeping in the stone." He himself is the sculptor. In carving the ideal man out of the crude materials of the present, he is guided by a "shadow" - the shadow of the Superman. He seems to feel that any destruction resulting from his creative act is justified: "Fragments fly from the stone: what is that to me?"

Comment

Zarathustra's mood is now affirmative and forceful. In the Prologue, he found himself casting about, first one way and then another, for a means of establishing communication with others. He attempted to appeal to the pride of his listeners, and when this did not work, he blamed himself. Now, however, he speaks of his "hammer" - he has found the tools with which to work. One of these tools is his present alliance of the doctrine that "God is dead" with the positive doctrine of the value of creative activity. This new ideal, replacing the "perfect and the unmoved," is the Superman, and the key to the new ideal is knowledge, will, and creation.

Of The Compassionate

Zarathustra defines man: he is "the animal with red cheeks," the animal that can feel shame. He extends his thesis that one should not cause one's enemy to feel shame (in Of the

Adder's Bite), to all persons. It is better, he says, to feel shame in the presence of the unfortunate, than to cause others to be ashamed. Zarathustra does not care for compassionate people who take pleasure in feeling sympathy for others. These, he says, "are lacking in shame." Men should learn, instead, how to enjoy themselves, a skill which will decrease the ways in which they may harm others. Zarathustra warns the "compassionate" that the imposition of an obligation upon another makes that other resentful, rather than grateful. The poor should be able to look upon it as an honor, to accept from the one who is rich. The spiritually rich (like Zarathustra himself) should not give, but should allow their riches to be taken. Such a relation among men will serve to reduce the amount of shame present in giving and taking.

Beggars, sinners, bad conscience, and petty thoughts are denounced, because they are the companions of shame. The outright and obvious evil deed is preferable, because it, at least, is a warning and a test of health. Zarathustra teaches that it is better to act wickedly, than to think petty thoughts. As he rejects compassion, he rejects pity. The antidote for pity, he says, is "great love."

Comment

Zarathustra condemns pity and compassion, but he does not intend to advocate brutality and an unfeeling approach to his fellow men. On the contrary, he is concerned with a very great problem in human relations, and he is trying to meet it head on. How may one treat one's neighbor feelingly, allowing him to benefit, without arousing shame and without debasing either party? Pity and compassion, he feels, go hand in hand with begging, self-indulgence, guilt, and petty resentment. But the self must remain intact, even as one man enriches another. This passage, therefore, depends upon the view expressed in The Bestowing Virtue: that there is a kind of selfishness which overflows to enrich the lives of others. This view has been called "enlightened egoism." Zarathustra comments, "I offer myself to my love, and my neighbor is myself." To repress one's selfish feelings "for the sake" of others is to produce guilt and bad conscience. But Zarathustra's demand is a hard one: it is to release such desires, among all unwelcome and embarrassing impulses, and to transform them so that they benefit others. This is "great love," and it is, unquestionably, a part of self-overcoming.

With this passage, it becomes clearer than ever that Nietszche's great concern is with human relations. The present passage is outstanding, because it ties together many threads of thought which were introduced in the first part of the book. One many express the view in this way: true morality among men must spring from an affirmation of oneself, never from a denial of oneself.

Of The Priests

Now Zarathustra turns his attention to those who have, he believes, made a morality of self-denial, the priests. He chides them for making a God out of the very forces that are harmful to them (see the later book, *The Genealogy of Morals*). These priests are "humble"; they look upon all men as "sinners"; they are ashamed of themselves; they dress in back, resembling corpses. Their values, however, are false, because they deny the nature of man: "He whom they call Redeemer has cast them ... into the bondage of false values."

Comment

Zarathustra reaffirms his conviction that true values cannot be found in a denial of natural impulses. Nature and morality must, instead, support one another. This is a necessary doctrine, when the supernatural is rejected ("God is dead"). The very buildings of the priests symbolically wall nature out. Truth will return only when "the clear sky again looks through broken roofs ...," that is, when the barriers between nature and morality are destroyed.

Of The Virtuous

Zarathustra warns his disciples not to seek rewards for virtuous behavior. There is no basis, he says, for expecting rewards for good actions, or punishment for bad ones. The idea that there are such "natural" rewards and punishments is a mistaken one, but nevertheless men have a tendency to believe it. Zarathustra hints that the belief has been "introduced" into the thought of men (a reference to religion). True virtue, he repeats, is an extension of the true self. Love of virtue is, then, as natural as love of self, or a mother's love for her child. There are, however, those who are falsely virtuous: those who find virtue in suffering, in their own laziness, in their own lacks, in whatever restrains their natural actions; those for whom virtue is mechanical, mere habit; and those for whom it is a "righteous" vengeance. Perhaps worst, however, are those for whom virtue lies in avoidance of all controversy, and in a consequent fear of action. It appears, in fact, that anything at all may seem to be a virtue, depending upon one's personal temper.

Zarathustra definitely rejects the idea that virtue lies in unselfishness, and affirms the belief that virtue lies in action which enriches the self. He concludes this discourse by assuring his friends that for each cast-down virtue, he will erect a new one in its place.

Comment

Now Zarathustra has expanded his list of "bad" values. In addition to the value "Pity," he now rejects a multitude of things that are regarded by many as virtues. All of these virtues may be seen as forms of denial of self, or of the "bad" form of selfishness. He also added to his condemnation of belief in a nonearthly, perfect condition (see Of the Afterworldsmen and Of the Blissful Isles), by rejecting the idea that there is a source of reward and punishment in the very nature of things; the universe is neither perfect nor moral. This is not an invitation to pessimism, however, because of the promise of new values to replace those which are lost when the moral interpretation of the universe is abandoned.

Of The Rabble

Zarathustra warns against the influence of those he calls "the rabble." Higher souls, becoming aware of the way in which the "rabble" spoil life, may begin to behave as though blind and deaf- simply to "cut out" the unpleasant "rabble." But he may be led to open his eyes and ears again by becoming aware of the impending "great Noontide." The sense of a future for man, the coming of the Superman, gives a meaning to life, and makes waiting a pleasure.

Comment

This passage is related to the previous discourses, Of the Flies of the Market Place and Of the New Idol. By "rabble," Nietzsche does not mean the common people (in contrast to the aristocracy), but rather all those who do not serve as a bridge to the Superman. These are the ones who have accepted the "ultimate man" as their ideal, and may include both priests and politicians. A fairly comprehensive picture of the "rabble" might be constructed, beginning with the intense social criticism given in Of the New Idol. The Superman, in contrast, is now clearly intended to be an ideal which is to serve as a guide to self-overcoming, to true virtue, and to give meaning to the present.

Of The Tarantulas

Zarathustra presents a vivid description of the tarantula, and the cave in which it lives. This spider, he says, is a symbol of the "preachers of equality." Those who preach equality, however, really do so out of a desire for revenge. He explains that this stems from an antagonism toward "all who are not as we are." The "tarantulas" are would-be tyrants, motivated by impotence, self-conceit, and envy. Their doctrine, however, may sometimes appear to be similar to that of Zarathustra himself, because they, too, turn against the "preachers of death" and are advocates of life and of earthly values. But their true nature is revealed by their desire to punish, by their conception of justice. The only reason they advocate life is their opposition to those presently in positions of power, but their doctrine, unlike Zarathustra's, would change with a change in conditions.

Zarathustra's own view is that men are not equal. Man's progress is achieved through a conflict of values, which, at bottom, is a conflict among men. Even in beauty, there is a necessary element of conflict. As he concludes this discourse, Zarathustra cries out that the tarantula has bitten him on the finger. But he refuses to take revenge upon the creature, and asks his friends to tie him to a pillar, rather than allow him to do so.

Comment.

The "tarantulas" represent "socialists." Their enemies, the "preachers of death," may be taken to be the priesthood, or the advocates of an "accepted" morality, who are in a position of power. Zarathustra interprets the Socialist doctrine of equality among men as the expression of a desire for revenge on the part of inferior persons against superior ones. Nietzsche held this interpretation of any point of view that places all men on the same "level." His comment that the spider has bitten him, and his refusal to strike back, are meant as a reference to the passage Of the Adder's Bite, in which he insisted that justice is not to be found in revenge.

Of The Famous Philosophers

Zarathustra accuses the "famous philosophers" of having subordinated their powers of thought to the superstitions of the crowd, rather than to the interest of truth. Philosophers may be admired by the masses, because they have tried to support the values of the crowd, but the true creator, the "free spirit," will be disliked and condemned, because he challenges the deepest superstitions of a culture. The people have identified "truth" with their own way of looking at things, and the "famous philosophers" have called the justification of their viewpoint the "will to truth." Such philosophers have, indeed, served a purpose, because they have tried to find a reasonable basis for the beliefs of the masses. But the truly creative spirit must know how to attack itself. Wisdom is propelled forward only by the free and fearless spirit.

Comment

The German philosopher Immanuel Kant (1724-1804) seems to be referred to here. Kant's entire system may be interpreted as a support for traditional morality. His theory raises the Golden Rule to the status of a "categorical imperative," which cannot be denied by any rational man. However, almost any philosopher, including Socrates, could be shown to have, in one way or another, supported traditional values. Even Nietzsche, despite his antagonism toward tradition, upholds many traditional values: love of family, of friendship, and hatred of revenge. But his attack, here, is not upon any specific values, but rather upon the assumption of fixity of values. Nietzsche's objection to the "famous philosophers" is that they help to keep values in a state of inflexibility by giving them a supposedly "rational" basis, and thereby restrict creativity in valuation, which he takes to be the most important factor in the progress of man.

The Night Song

Zarathustra sings of the loneliness of the man who gives to others, but who cannot take from them. He speaks of the "wretchedness of all givers," which is the solitude that comes to the one who is a source and a creator of benefits. It is the solitude of the mother, opposed to the companionship-in mutual need-of the sucklings. Such loneliness is a danger, because it may lead the creative one to lose his humility, and the natural desire for companionship may develop into a desire to take from others. But the solitude of the creative spirit cannot be alleviated, even by seeking out other creative souls, because the givers must all follow their own paths. It is not easy for them to communicate, even among themselves. Such givers are, indeed, like "many suns"; "to all that is dark they speak with their light-to me they are silent."

Comment

This is the first of three poetic songs, which have been taken to be autobiographical in content. Here, Nietzsche expresses his own personal solitude, his own lack of communication with others. Following as it does, the passage Of the Famous Philosophers, it serves to emphasize his own feeling of isolation, even from other great intellects. However, the autobiographical interpretation does not exhaust the meaning of the discourse. Nietzsche has, in fact, touched upon a real problem. In *The Bestowing Virtue*, he spoke of a "selfishness" that is a virtue, because it produces a "natural" flow of benefit to others. But if this "enlightened" selfishness brings with it an unlooked-for isolation from others, then it threatens to destroy itself. Perhaps, however, this "paradox of the bestowing virtue" may be solved: Zarathustra says, "a gulf stands between giving and receiving; and the smallest gulf must be bridged at last." But he does not specify how this is to be accomplished.

The Dance Song

Zarathustra and his disciples come upon a group of girls, dancing in the woods. When the girls stop dancing, he urges them to continue, explaining that he is no "spoil-sport." He says that he, himself, is like a "forest and a night of dark trees," within which one may find the "little God" beloved by all girls, the God Cupid. As the girls resume their play, Zarathustra sings of his own two "mistresses," Life and Wisdom. Life is a deep abyss into which Zarathustra would sink, but he is pulled up by Life's "golden rod." Wisdom, like Life, is difficult to fathom, and also has a golden rod. Both are like women, changeable, defiant, and seductive. Yet Life appears to take precedence: "I am fond of Wisdom ... because she reminds me of Life."

Evening comes, and Zarathustra is seized by melancholy. The gay mood of the dance has passed, and Zarathustra cries out, "Why? Wherefore? Whereby? Whither? Where? How? Is it not folly to go on living?" Even he cannot escape moments of sadness.

Comment

In this section, Zarathustra likens himself to the night, yet in The Night Song, he was like the sun, opposed to "all that is dark." This contrast shows that the soul of the giver is complex: more than one **metaphor** may describe it. In the discourse Of the Compassionate, Zarathustra speaks of two modes of giving: one may give "gladly as a friend to friends," but "strangers and the poor may pluck the fruit from my tree for themselves." While both methods of giving are involuntary (the "natural overflow"), the first is active, and may be associated with the sun, which radiates its warmth. There are both active and passive modes of giving; the giver is both a "sun" and a "tree."

The "golden rod" of Life and Wisdom is a symbol of power, and recalls the staff, which was given to Zarathustra by his disciples, and upon which was a serpent, the symbol of Wisdom.

The Funeral Song

This is a song of lament for the joys of youth. Zarathustra speaks of his youthful experiences as his "dead ones." He praises his memories as riches; but he condemns his enemies, who have destroyed his youthful ideals. Yet he has managed to survive, through his strength of will.

Comment

This passage, also, has been taken as autobiographical, and may refer, in part, to the composer Richard Wagner, a friend whom Nietzsche later condemned, but in whom he had placed much faith. In general, however, Nietzsche speaks against any who hold out false promises and false ideals. Only the strength of will can sustain one, when the visions of youth are destroyed.

Of Self-Overcoming

Now Zarathustra discusses his doctrine of the will to power in more detail. Wise men believe they are following a "will to truth" in seeking new values; but actually, they desire to bring all existence under a code of understanding, and this is the manifestation, rather, of a will to power. All living things must necessarily undergo some form of obedience. To escape subjection to the command of others, a creature must become capable of commanding itself. Such self command, however, presupposes self-obedience. Command of oneself is the greatest responsibility, and requires the greatest obedience. But self-obedience and self-command, in freeing an individual from the command of others, are the highest forms of the will to power. Self-overcoming and the will to power, then, are the same.

Self-overcoming is also the key to creativity, and creativity is a manifestation of power, both constructive and destructive.

Comment

It is evident that by "power" Nietzsche does not mean "brute force." Power manifests itself in the creation of values, and this, in turn, is a result of self-overcoming (refer to Of the Thousand and One Goals). It is for the sake of life, and the perpetuation of life, that creation of values takes place, and the power of the creator is the power to preserve life. But life is not a static thing, and therefore the stability of the "ultimate man" is really a form of death, a denial of life, and a lack of power. The will to power is a will to continue life in a creative sense, and self-overcoming is its touchstone.

Although Nietzsche has here introduced the doctrine of the "will of power," and linked it with self-overcoming, the ideas presented have only a loose, informal structure. There is no clear-cut meaning for the important terms "obedience," "command," and "power." It would be premature, however, to ask for precision of definition. Nietzsche is "writing with blood," and his meaning has to be felt, perhaps, before it can be "understood" in an intellectual sense. This is not to say, however, that Nietzsche's meaning is obscure or wholly personal. His references to "obedience" and "command," which may be related to his account of "the spirit of the camel," are clearly psychological notions associated with the idea of sublimation (self-overcoming), and are not to be placed in any "military" context. Nietzsche has, indeed, said a great deal: life is not the mere struggle for existence, and it is not submission to an externally imposed morality; it is the will to power. But what is the will to power? He replies: it is to be found in self-obedience, self-command, true individuality, and the creation of new values in a changing world; discover these, and you will have discovered the will to power.

Of The Sublime Men

Zarathustra turns his critical eye upon those who, in their search for truth, ignore laughter, beauty, and the pleasures of the earth. He does not care for these "penitent" men, pale men, who fear the sunlight. These "sublime men" have too much control over themselves, in the sense that their strength of will prevents them from releasing the natural instincts which must be sublimated, rather than repressed. There is, indeed, a "wild beast" lurking within the sublime man, which must be overcome, and therefore released. Yet the sublime man is a man of power; he needs, however, to free his will, and to reach a serenity which is not opposed to the beauty of life. He must eventually hold a mirror up to his own beauty, and when his will has been freed of the burden of keeping natural instincts at bay, there may appear a glimpse, "in dreams," of the "superhero." Beauty, Zarathustra says, is power which has descended into the visible.

Comment

This passage serves as a clarification of the notion of "obedience." The man who has overcome himself is not one who, like the priests and "despisers of the body," rejects the earthly life. Nor is he like the "famous philosophers" who praise intellectual rationalization as a "will to truth." Obedience, then, does not mean suppression of natural instincts and rigid adherence to a rule of reason. His reference to the paleness of the sublime man recalls the definition of man as "the animal with red cheeks";

laughter, shame, emotions of the heart: these are more important than gravity and an intellectual scowl. In the sublime man, these valuable passions are suppressed, rather than sublimated. Self-overcoming aims at the release, direction, and control of the passions, not their suppression. In connecting sublimation with beauty, Nietzsche recalls *The Birth of Tragedy*: The descent of power into the visible, the reflection in the mirror, the approach of the superhero in dreams - these all may be likened to the Apollonian imposition of form upon the formlessness of the unreasoning emotions. Such a "forming" is a control through **imagery**, not through rational suppression. Obedience and self-overcoming, then, are related to the concept of Apollonian beauty. The free expression of the desire for pleasure, in a controlled, imaginative form, can produce a sense of beauty. The philosopher George Santayana defines beauty as "pleasure objectified" (in *The Sense of Beauty*, Dover Publications, New York, 1955).

Of The Land Of Culture

Zarathustra criticizes contemporary men, who boast of their "**realism**" and their lack of superstition. He condemns this "pride" as a sign of barrenness; those who lack belief are unable to create belief, and therefore condemn everything. Zarathustra is thankful that he is able to laugh at these men, for otherwise, he says, he would become sick. He finds no substance in them, no core of being, but only a patchwork of many cultures and values.

Comment

This is a resumption of the attack on nihilism, the lack of belief in any values at all. Particularly notable, however, is the fact that Nietzsche links nihilism to a lack of cultural unity-a view which he expressed in *The Birth of Tragedy* by pointing out that modern man has lost his unifying "myth." That this comment follows immediately the reference to dreams and images in Of the Sublime Men reinforces the connection of the idea of sublimation with the idea of the Apollonian. Sublimation creates values; therefore it opposes nihilism.

Of Immaculate Perception

Here, the sublime man and the nihilist are linked. The man who believes in "pure knowledge" and "contemplation," but denies the importance of the earthly emotions, must feel shame in his own existence, because he is living a lie; he does not believe in himself.

Comment

Here Zarathustra criticizes a theory of knowledge that looks upon knowledge as a mere passive reflection of things that are already complete in themselves; the knowing man is thought of as a simple mirror, like the moon, which merely reflects the light of the sun. But even the moon produces a change in the quality of the light reflected, and perhaps no mirror can reflect "perfectly," without changing the reflected image. Zarathustra, acknowledging this, asserts the necessity of a creative element in knowing. A theory that makes man, as knower, into a mere passive mirror of events, leaves out (in theory) what is always present (in fact): man as evaluator. Such a view, then, will always miss the mark. In Of the Thousand and One Goals, Zarathustra stated, "Without evaluation the nut of existence would be hollow." In the present discourse, he says, "... this I call knowledge: all that is deep shall rise up-to my height!" He repeats, then, the message in Of the Afterworldsmen, that the creating self is both the value and the measure of things.

Of Scholars

An especially distasteful sort of "mirrorknower" is derided by Zarathustra in this sharply barbed passage: the "scholars" who desire to be simple "spectators." Their worst trait is that they dislike originality, and desire, like the "tarantulas," to place all intellects on the same level. To this end, they even mistrust one another; they "lie in wait like spiders." But Zarathustra compares them to sheep, and says that they value only the most superficial signs of knowledge.

Of Poets

Zarathustra turns his attack upon poets, including even himself. The criticism is in a humorous vein, but there is a serious side to it. Poetry is not a special source of knowledge, and too often it holds out false promises of wisdom (see *The Funeral Song*). Poets often assume reality to be "unattainable," and this, to Zarathustra, is tiresome. Poetic **metaphor** also lends itself to unclarity. A kind of nihilism, a "penitent spirit," may even overtake the poet, who may become weary of an apparently fruitless striving.

Comment

Zarathustra has now completed a series of descriptions, beginning with Of the Sublime Men, of those who might be taken for Supermen, but are not. Now, however, events are about to take their own course. The sequence of sustained and somewhat arrogant sarcasm is about to be jolted by an omen from the skies, strange events, and sailor's tales. Even Zarathustra is not exempt from the contingencies of Fate.

Of Great Events

Zarathustra is away from "the Blissful Isles" on an investigation of his own. A ship anchors nearby, and the sailors are startled to see an image, resembling Zarathustra himself, soaring over their heads in the direction of a nearby volcano. The image speaks, crying: "It is time!" It is high time!" The sailors tell Zarathustra's followers about this strange sign in the heavens. At first, there is concern for Zarathustra himself, but he returns, safely, after five days. He has been "visiting" the volcano, and he tells of his conversation with this "fire-dog." The volcano is a symbol of revolutionary spirits, who desire to bring about important changes by means of vast social upheavals. Zarathustra, however, belittles those who, like the volcano, make a great noise about things. Great changes take place quietly, in "our stillest hours."

The disciples, however, pay little attention to Zarathustra's story, because they are very excited about the vision of the sailors. When they tell Zarathustra of this vision, he is perplexed, and not a little concerned. He identifies the image as his "shadow," but he is unable to understand its message. He asks, "For what, then, is it-high time?"

Comment

The shadow is a sign of the future, and of the ideal toward which Zarathustra must strive. It is a messenger of change, and a warning to Zarathustra that he must not turn away from his true course. Zarathustra, however, does not perceive clearly what this course may be, and he becomes increasingly disturbed by the vision.

The Prophet

Zarathustra hears the voice of a prophet of pessimism, who foretells a time of futility, in which all efforts will come to nothing. This produces a feeling of grief and weariness in Zarathustra. He fasts for three days, and then falls asleep. When he awakens, he describes a terrifying nightmare. In this dream, Zarathustra, having turned away from life, becomes a guard for "death's coffins." With an oppressed soul, he enters behind great doors, carrying his guard's keys, and there he stays in an atmosphere of heavy and malignant quietude. Suddenly, a great sound rocks the chamber; three knocks on the door, and three again. He struggles to open the door, but cannot. A fierce wind, however, tears the door away, and a coffin is blown in. The coffin opens, letting out a myriad of strange creatures, both fair and foul. Zarathustra is filled with horror. At this point, the dream ends.

The disciples attempt to interpret the dream. One of them suggests that the "wind" is Zarathustra himself, and the coffin of gay things, perhaps, is Zarathustra's doctrine. Zarathustra appears to take heart, but inwardly he remains puzzled.

Comment

The "prophet" in this passage may represent the philosopher Schopenhauer, whose doctrine that life is a mere will to exist was rejected in the discourse Of Self-overcoming. The door, which Zarathustra cannot open himself, represents the way to the doctrine of eternal recurrence. This doctrine, which Zarathustra must eventually expound, has a fearsome as well as a beneficial aspect, and for this reason, it has not yet found its way to Zarathustra's conscious mind. He is, in fact, repressing the doctrine, keeping it hidden from himself because of his fear of it, and therefore he is disturbed by dreams and visions.

Of Redemption

In a scene that resembles the allegory of the tightrope walker, in the Prologue, Zarathustra is surrounded by beggars as he crosses a bridge. A hunchback steps forth, and asks Zarathustra to cure them all of their infirmities. Zarathustra replies that the cripple, who has learned to live with his problem, may be thrown "off balance," if subjected to a sudden cure. Then, perhaps, he will curse the one who has healed him. There is a worse sort of cripple, Zarathustra points out: the imbalanced personality. He calls these the "inverse cripples," and caricatures them as men who have developed one faculty to the exclusion of all others: "... men who are no more than a great eye or a great mouth or a great belly. ..." Such "inverse cripples" are sometimes mistaken for great men, but Zarathustra says they are not great, merely grotesque.

The real cripples and beggars, however, trouble Zarathustra, who turns bitterly to his disciples, saying: "I walk among men as among the fragments ... Of men." He is brought, thereby, to meditate upon the shortcomings of men. The greatest burden, he says, is the knowledge that the past cannot be changed. The will to change the past is faced with an impossible condition, for the past cannot be altered. Such a frustrated will, desiring revenge, may eventually turn against itself, and the extreme of this process leads to the nihilistic conclusion that all life is punishment.

Comment

The error of interpreting the world in terms of reward and punishment has already been pointed out in the discourse Of the Virtuous. In The Funeral Song, Zarathustra invoked his strength of will as the quality which has prevented him from becoming despondent about past failures. In that passage, he also used such terms as "eternity" and "resurrections," which serve as a hint of the doctrine of eternal recurrence. The need for a source of "redemption" from the past, and the finding of this redemption in the will, are now uppermost, because this is the issue which calls for the new doctrine. Zarathustra, however, is still not ready to explain this doctrine (even to himself). Instead, he asks a question: How shall the will of the Superman reconcile itself with Time? Is it possible to "will backwards"? Zarathustra, unable to answer this, ends his discourse. But the hunchback, who has heard the entire discussion, suggests that Zarathustra is not yet finished; he has more to say, but only to himself. This hunchback, and the "prophet" of the previous discourse, are simply different forms of the "shadow" of Zarathustra; each time, they act as a catalyst, to push him closer to the new doctrine. Such "catalyst" - figures, for example, a magician or a dwarf, often appear in fairy tales as messengers of change, pointing out the path which must be followed, but seldom revealing the true nature of the goal. (See the writings of the Swiss psychologist C. G. Jung.)

Of Manly Prudence

Zarathustra's shock at the "fragments" of men which surround him, and the hunchback's suggestion that he is not quite being honest with himself, lead him to meditate upon his own position among the rest of mankind. He stands between man and the Superman, as if between an abyss and the limitless heavens; but he must have an anchor, a place to rest his hand. Therefore he lives among men as a matter of prudence. And it is, indeed, his "manly prudence" which leads him to accept vanity, deception, and wickedness in man. He will, therefore, remain among men, disguised, and not attempting to understand, but rather to misunderstand them-if only so that he can bear the present state of things.

Comment

This suggestion, that he who reaches to the heights must have an anchor, is a comment upon the relation of ideals to the material out of which they may be realized; the relation of theory to practice. Zarathustra must cling to man, because man is the real means to the Superman. He sees that no ideal can be realized without the material out of which it is to be built. The unsettled state of material which is "in transition" is no reason for condemning it, even though its "incomplete" state may be bothersome, at times, to the one who looks ahead. To accept this necessary aspect of progress is "manly prudence." Such a view is in harmony with the doctrines of philosophical pragmatism.

The Stillest Hour

Zarathustra confronts his friends with the news that he must leave them once again. He has had yet another dream, in which a voice, unable to convince Zarathustra that he is ready to "take command," orders him to return to his solitude until he becomes prepared for this step. This is the "stillest hour," and even though Zarathustra feels that he has not succeeded in reaching the people, the dream voice says, "The dew falls upon the grass when the night is most silent."

Comment

In this manner, the second part ends as did the first, with Zarathustra's voluntary retirement into solitude. Now, however, he goes with a great responsibility upon his shoulders. He must "take command" of himself, so that his new doctrine may emerge in a healthy form. The voice of "the stillest hour" recalls the discourse Of Great Events, where it was pointed out that revolutions occur quietly. The comment about "falling dew" is a reference to Zarathustra's own remark in Of the Flies of the Market Place, that small things such as "raindrops and weeds" may bring about great results.

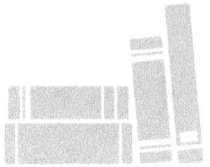

THUS SPOKE ZARATHUSTRA

TEXTUAL ANALYSIS

PART 3

The Wanderer

Zarathustra now begins his journey from the Blissful Islands to his mountain retreat. He crosses the mountain ridge of the island, making for the harbor on the other side. His mood is one of sorrow, fear, and anticipation. He knows that his last and greatest test lies before him. He welcomes this promise of danger, however, because it is a part of his calling. (Thus once again he recalls the Prologue, and his own comments to the dying acrobat.)

Comment

In this passage, Zarathustra makes a puzzling combination of statements. He remarks, at first, that in the final analysis, one can only experience oneself. Then, a moment later, he expresses the thought that clear sight only comes in looking away from oneself. How can this apparent contradiction be reconciled? How can one look away from oneself, if it is true that ultimately one experiences only that self? There are two facets of this question, a philosophical one, and a psychological one. Nietzsche has hinted at the philosophical issue earlier, in suggesting that the ego is the measure of all things; for if this is so, how can there be any knowledge of a common reality, which is the same to all men? This deep philosophical problem is one which is raised especially by the German philosopher Kant, but it can be traced throughout the entire history of philosophy.

The psychological question is a curious one. It is closely linked to the problem of self-overcoming. Even the phrase "self-overcoming" suggests a contradiction: how is it that the self may overcome itself? Plato had presented the problem of virtue as a problem of the relation of one part of the self to another, but here there is no question of parts in conflict. This is, in fact, the question of the possibility (and the value) of seeing ourselves as others see us-of somehow "getting outside" of ourselves. Some, indeed, have taken the apparent impossibility of this as evidence that life itself is contradictory, and therefore irrational. In *The Birth of Tragedy*, Nietzsche speaks of the mystical contradiction of the Dionysian "reality" - the union of the self with the universe, or the not-self.

It is out of "contradictions" like these that philosophical problems have always arisen, and such "contradictions" seem to call for an "analysis of concepts," or, as Socrates took it, a search for a definition. Here the question is raised, what is meant by "Self"? There is much in *Thus Spoke Zarathustra* to indicate that Nietzsche looked upon the traditional concept of the Self as limited, and in need of reappraisal. He calls for a new Self, a new will a new pride (see Of the Afterworldsmen), and a new idea of "selfishness." Nietzsche has said that the Self is the body. It is, then, not an isolated thing which must reach out for an external reality. It is, instead, a part of reality (see Of the Despisers of the Body). This view, however, is a controversial one; but one thing does stand out: the Self which does "overcome" itself attains a special power. So Zarathustra, in the present discourse, says that looking down upon himself is his "summit."

Of The Vision And The Riddle

After boarding the ship which is to take him to the mainland, Zarathustra remains silent for two days. Finally, sensing that his fellow passengers are adventurers like himself, he speaks to them of a vision, the "vision of the most solitary man." In this vision, Zarathustra walks through a twilight land, up a difficult path, carrying an unpleasant creature-half dwarf, half mole-upon his shoulders. This creature, whom he names the Spirit of Gravity, mocks Zarathustra, saying, "You have thrown yourself high, but every stone that is thrown must-fall!" The dwarf then stops speaking. Both the mockery and the silence of the Spirit of Gravity disturb Zarathustra. Finally, he draws upon his courage, and challenges the dwarf. But the miserable creature leaps from his shoulders, for a gateway stands at the place where they have halted. A thought occurs to Zarathustra which "lightens" him. He says that the name of the gateway is "Moment." Behind them, the past extends eternally. Since it is eternal, all things that have happened once must have happened before, and indeed over and over again, an infinite number of times.

The dwarf and the gateway disappear at his words, and he stands alone. Suddenly he sees a man, a young shepherd, sprawled upon the ground. A black snake has crawled into the shepherd's mouth and is choking the poor man. Zarathustra, horrified, cries out "Bite! Bite!," and the shepherd bites off the head of the snake and then spits it out. Released from his antagonist, the man springs to his feet, laughing like a man transformed.

Comment

The "Spirit of Gravity" represents nihilism, in all the forms in which Zarathustra has presented it: as the "penitent spirit," the "spirit of revenge," and the "prophet." The dwarf's comment, that "every stone that is thrown must-fall", expresses the nihilistic belief that no worthwhile goal can be attained. In particular, however, the dwarf represents the nihilism that arises when the will is frustrated by the unchangeable nature of the past (see Of Redemption).

Zarathustra, then, is confronted (in the vision) by nihilism itself, the very embodiment of his archenemy. He has been led to announce the doctrine of eternal recurrence, even though this has only taken place in a vision. But a strange thing has happened: the Spirit of Gravity, his enemy, appears to agree with this doctrine, and itself says that "time ... is a circle." Even in the earlier passage Of Redemption, it was the "spirit of revenge," not Zarathustra, who used the phrase "eternally recurring deed." What, then, has Zarathustra to add to this nihilism of the will which is frustrated by Time? There is no answer here, only the vision of the man with the snake in his mouth. In Of Redemption, Zarathustra spoke of the will which must will something higher than mere reconciliation with Time, and there he asked, "How shall that happen?" The act of the shepherd, biting off the head of the snake to free himself, is a symbolic expression of the answer to this problem. At this point, then, the solution is not made clear, but is left in allegorical form. The full **exposition** of this vision will come in a later chapter, The Convalescent.

Of Involuntary Bliss

Zarathustra affirms that what is still lacking is a final self-overcoming. Recalling the passage Of Marriage and Children, he says that he has an obligation to perfect himself, for the sake of his "children." (These are his doctrines and his new values, to which he "gives birth.") He now interprets all the dreams and visions of the preceding sections as symbols of the need for his own final self-perfection. He must summon up, and overcome, his own deepest thought. He has reached a state of "pregnancy," and even though he now feels a premature happiness, he bids this "involuntary bliss" to leave him, for he knows that his greatest test is yet to come.

Before Sunrise

Zarathustra praises the sky, as a symbol of this doctrine that rationality and "eternal will" are not the limits of the universe, and that there is also chance, freedom, and "a little foolishness" in all things. Like the sky, the universe itself is not entirely bounded by rules or laws. Especially, he denies that events in the universe are representative of a moral order of things. From an "eternal" point of view, events are "beyond" good and evil. But the sky which Zarathustra praises is a morning twilight sky. The sun has yet to rise.

Of The Virtue That Makes Small

Zarathustra leaves the ship when it arrives at the mainland, but he does not seek out his mountain retreat at once. Instead, he travels among the populace, in order to see the present state of things. He finds that the people are afraid of him, and that they are growing "smaller" because of their belief in moderation. They call moderation a virtue, but Zarathustra calls it mediocrity and cowardice. He now proclaims himself "Zarathustra the Godless." He urges the people to assert their own will, and to reject "moderation," which is a form of submission. He announces that the "great Noontide" is near, and that those who make a virtue of avoiding the deeper parts of their spirit will wither and die.

On The Mount Of Olives

Again Zarathustra speaks to the sky, but this time it is the sky of winter. It is good, he says, to bear the cold, and not to flee from it. Others may pity him, and some may envy him, for his self-imposed chilly solitude. But he remains like the winter sky, wrapped in a "long, luminous silence." He has learned to hide the "sun" of his wisdom to keep unworthy men from basking, unwelcome, in its light. This passage is a restatement of the **theme** that one must not fail to face even the most uncomfortable truths about oneself, even if it means a cold solitude, which others cannot understand.

Of Passing By

Zarathustra continues on his way back to the mountain. He comes to a city gate. but a fool blocks his way. This man is called "Zarathustra's ape," because he imitates Zarathustra's own manner. The fool warns Zarathustra away from the city, and begins a criticism of its inhabitants that is very like the criticism given earlier in Of the New Idol. But Zarathustra rejects the fool, saying that the fool criticizes from the worst of motives: revenge. Zarathustra says that his own contempt of the values of the city dwellers arises out of love, and it is meant as a warning to them. So saying, he passes the city by, because he feels no love for it.

Of The Apostates

Another sort of unfortunate, the man who has abandoned Zarathustra's teaching and has returned to religion, is now taken to task. Some of Zarathustra's early followers have failed to show the sort of strength and endurance which is necessary, and have reverted to religious piety. Zarathustra says that the truth is that there is no God, and therefore these men must fear the truth. They are like fishermen who fish in a barren pond, and this, he believes, is so ridiculous that he will not even dignify it by calling it "superficial."

The Homecoming

Now the wanderer returns to his mountain home, and he speaks to it, calling it his Solitude. The course of his many journeys is recalled, and he realizes that among men he has been lonely. Now, however, he is able to communicate, with himself and with his Solitude. He was tempted to remain among men because of pity, but this soon turned into self-deception, because the truth about men is difficult to endure (see Of Manly Prudence). Finally, he learned even to conceal himself. Now, however, returned to his Solitude and with no need for deception, he welcomes the freedom which he finds upon the mountain peak. For the while, he will speak only to himself.

Of The Three Evil Things

Zarathustra considers three things which have been looked upon, before now, as evil: sensual pleasure, lust for power, and selfishness. He asks himself: what is their true value? Sensual pleasure, while it is a burden for the "rabble" and a goad to the "despisers of the body," is a medicine to the Superman. In it, Zarathustra sees a key to the meaning of activity. Sensual pleasure can be "an overflowing of thanks to the present from all the future." It is, in other words, a natural part of the aim and fulfillment of effort, and in the healthy man it should be admitted as such.

Lust for power, he says, can destroy the man who is not truly powerful. But in the Superman, the exercise of power is no longer a lust, but a natural overflow. Zarathustra recalls that he has spoken of this as "the bestowing virtue."

Selfishness, also, can be a virtue - the selfishness which is truly identical with the gathering of power called "self-overcoming." The mark of such a selfish one is that he looks upon his happiness as his good, and upon all that is cowardly, submissive, and "pious" as his bad. The "three evil things," therefore, can be virtues, but they can only be so for the man who has overcome himself. In the souls of the "rabble," they are still evils. He concludes by predicting the arrival of the "great Noontide," in which a transformation of values will take place.

Of The Spirit Of Gravity

Zarathustra recalls that creature, half mole, half dwarf, which perched upon his shoulders in an earlier vision, and which he called "the Spirit of Gravity." This creature represents that acute form of pessimism called nihilism, and in the present passage, Zarathustra becomes more specific about the nature of this malady. The seeds of nihilism are sown early in life. These "seeds" are the elements of the moral interpretation of the universe, which places the source of good and evil outside of men, and therefore presents all men with a common good and evil. This is the morality of the "natural" reward and punishment, which Zarathustra criticized in Of the Virtuous. The basic features of this moral interpretation of existence are the notions that existence is something for which we must be forgiven, that loving ourselves is the worst thing we can do, and that life is necessarily a burden. For this reason, the source of nihilism is called "the Spirit of Gravity": it makes of life, and of the earth, the heaviest of burdens. This "weighting-down" of life in earliest youth has two results: First, it encourages the feeling that life is a "desert." Second, it causes a growing repression of many truths about one's own self.

For this reason, one of the remedies for nihilism is self-acceptance and self-overcoming. (But this is not all that is necessary. The discourse Of the Vision and the Riddle has indicated that the doctrine of eternal recurrence must also be accepted. The way in which this is to be accomplished has yet to be divulged.)

Of Old And New Law Tables

Now Zarathustra waits upon the mountain side for the hour of his new "down-going," and for a new wisdom. Since he is now alone, he speaks only to himself. The present discourse is a recapitulation of his teachings. Mankind, he muses, does not know the true nature of good and evil. Only a creator of earthly values can supply the truth. The Spirit of Gravity, which brings about nihilism, still holds men down. But this is not entirely bad, if the dogmatic atmosphere of this "Spirit" is seen to be only a necessary point of transition. Man is, as he has said, a bridge, rather than a goal, and therefore all his shortcomings may be placed in a perspective of change; nothing is final (see Of Manly Prudence). The redemption of man is presented as a riddle: man must come to create the past. This riddle is not explained here, but it represents a desire that the past and the future should merge in some way. Obviously, this riddle is to be solved by the doctrine of "eternal recurrence."

Self-overcoming is demanded of all men. One should demand it of one's neighbor, as well as of oneself. Those of noble soul should seek the hard way, and not expect any more of life than they are willing to give to it. We must sacrifice ourselves for the sake of ourselves-our future selves. Only out of such a process can a new truth arise, and this creative process requires the dismissal of bad conscience and an admission of the "evil" as well as the good (see Of the Tree on the Mountainside).

What has been known, in the past, as "good" and "evil," is not unchangeable. Nothing in the world, including values, is fixed forever. People want to believe that there is no value, unless it is eternal, and thereby a secure foundation for life. But nature does not exhibit this kind of security. Nature is change; yet it is not wholly irrational. Values, therefore, must be based upon a knowledge of changing nature. Only science, not "prophets and astrologers," can supply the sort of knowledge that is necessary. A true psychology, for example, shows us that stealing and killing are a part of life, and their denial only denies life itself. (Such things may be overcome; but they cannot be denied.)

A "new nobility," or a new basis for dignity in human relations, is one of the aims toward which the Superman leads us. This is not a "nobility" in the ordinary sense of the word, but one which will arise out of self-overcoming. (Men must honor one another as a natural result of their own inner riches, not because they have been told to do so, or because of the fear of a "future" punishment.) A man should be honored for what he may become, not for what he has been, or what his predecessors have been. The possession of money is no basis for honor, either: "All that has price is of little value." Look to the future, Zarathustra demands; this is the one means of redeeming the past.

The doctrine that all is vain, that all purposes turn to nothing, because there is no eternal purpose (nihilism), is a doctrine for children, not for men. Life is a challenge to be met, not to be feared or denied. The living of life is enough. Disgust with the world creates a disgusting world; but it need not be so. Man must change the world, not submit to it, and not renounce it. To the nihilist, even knowledge is a bad thing, because he seeks to know "ultimate" things, and must grow weary of doing so. But true knowledge is a means to creation, and to the exercise of the will in new ways. It is, therefore, a liberating factor in life, rather than a binding factor. Knowledge is a means, not an end (see the criticism of the "mirror" view of knowledge in Of Immaculate Perception).

Zarathustra issues a challenge to all nihilists: if they are truly "world weary," they should leave this life. To continue to live, and to condemn life at the same time, is the sheerest hypocrisy. Even if they will not leave, however, they must soon pass away, whether they want to or not. The man who fights to overcome his weariness is to be honored and protected. The wisdom that comes with an affirmation of life and a rejection of nihilism is a wisdom that can be achieved only through individual effort. The man who tries to reach wisdom through the accomplishments of others is a parasite, and is to be condemned.

Zarathustra's doctrine is a hard one. The nihilists and the "parasites" must be condemned, and helped to their own destruction, because they are the enemies of the man who is to come. Some, however, are not even worthy of being enemies (the "rabble"). These are to be passed by. The "shopkeeper" culture is one of the things to be bypassed. Dancing and laughter are more important than the values of the market place.

Zarathustra turns his attention to the problems of marriage. Better no marriage at all, he says, than a bad one. He advocates, therefore, trial marriages. The decision to live together for an entire lifetime is not one which should be made lightly and without experience. Just as a marriage of couples is an experiment, so should the "marriage" of larger groups - those we call societies-be looked upon as experimental. Human relations should not be viewed as "contracts" among men, but as a series of great experiments, subject to change with a change in conditions, and not bound by any fixed dogma which may turn community life itself into a "bad marriage." For this reason, those who (like the "ultimate man") claim to know the "good and the just" once and for all, are a danger to a healthy society. But the abandoning of a fixed foundation, and the acceptance of a world of change, are terrifying. Therefore, the man-to-come must be strong. His strength, however, is the strength of self-overcoming, not of physical might.

Comment

It is now possible to list some of the value judgments which Zarathustra has presented:

1. Only earthly values are true values (values based upon a "supernatural" structure are condemned).

2. Nihilism is a stage of transition, not a final condition.

3. One should not expect any more from life than one puts into it.

4. Individuals should live a life of continual self-development.

5. Values should be based upon a knowledge of changing nature, not upon dreamlike ideals.

6. Men should not honor one another out of fear, nor out of a desire for reward, but out of a natural respect for other creative souls.

7. The most valuable things cannot be given a price. True riches are to be found in human relations and in self-development. Motives of revenge, reward, and punishment are a poor basis for human relations.

8. Life should not be feared, but accepted as a challenge.

9. Knowledge is to be valued as a means to life, and as an aid to self-development, but not as an all-powerful "oracle."

10. Nihilists who continue to live are hypocrites, and are to be condemned as enemies. If anyone is truly "morally bad," it is the nihilist.

11. Overemphasis upon the economic life of man is a bad thing. The arts and emotions are more important.

12. There should be trial marriages, as well as trial social institutions.

The Convalescent

Zarathustra is seized by a sudden madness, and he calls upon the deepest thoughts within him to come forth. This effort, however, is very great, and he falls into a stupor. His animals, the eagle and the serpent, watch over his slumbering form for seven days. After this period, he arises, and his animals ask if some new wisdom has disturbed his soul. He replies strangely, bidding the animals to continue their speech. He says that their words are like music, which appears to bring together "things eternally separated." Every soul, he says, is a unique world, and no soul can get outside of itself. Yet music helps one to overcome this condition.

The animals then continue to speak, and they restate the doctrine of eternal recurrence. The keynote of the doctrine is: "Existence begins in every instant." Zarathustra praises them, saying that it was indeed just this doctrine that had to come forth in him for a full acceptance. Now he makes clear the meaning of the vision of the shepherd with the snake in his mouth (in Of the Vision and the Riddle). The snake represented the doctrine of eternal recurrence, which had to be accepted. But its acceptance would have destroyed Zarathustra, had he not "bit off its head." This act symbolizes his final rejection of nihilism. The doctrine of eternal recurrence implies that all the evil in man, as well as the good, will also recur again and again, and this knowledge of the recurrence of evil as well as good has to be accepted, before the doctrine can bring true redemption.

Zarathustra again refers to music and song. To "sing again" - this he calls a comfort which he has devised for himself, in the face of nihilistic disgust at the evil in man. He accepts the task of teaching this doctrine, and this, he says, will be the end of his "down-going."

Comment

This is a clear reference to the **theme** of *The Birth of Tragedy*. The spirit of music affords a control over the Dionysian wisdom, which permits one to transcend individuality, without actually destroying his identity. In this way, Nietzsche shows that the comforting aspect of the aesthetic experience is still a high value for man, even if it is not now taken to be the ultimate goal. It is still not clear, however, how the doctrine of eternal recurrence constitutes a "redemption." Three points may be made in this connection, however: (1) Acceptance of eternal recurrence is only a redemption if nihilism has been overcome, and man's shortcomings have been given equal status with his virtues. (2) Eternal recurrence teaches that one lives again, so that the fear of death is abolished (but this is open to criticism, on the grounds that such a rebirth is no more than the same life all over again, not a continuance of life). (3) The doctrine suggests that each moment of life is precious, a "new beginning." This, perhaps, is the heart of the matter. To live as if this present life will be repeated eternally, requires that every moment be given all the meaning possible, so that only the best will be repeated. In this way, the doctrine may be looked upon as a supreme affirmation of the value of life.

Of The Great Longing

Zarathustra sings, now, to his own soul. He has given it a freedom from shame, from sinful guilt. He has purged from it the spirit of revenge, and brought it close to nature. Both future and past come together in his soul. But there is sorrow and melancholy in such fullness of soul, and the soul that will not weep must sing.

Comment

The idea that the future and the past "come together" in the free soul may be interpreted as a reference to the previous notion, that each moment is of great importance. Zarathustra realizes that such a doctrine does not mean merely living from moment to moment, disconnectedly, but rather seeing each moment in all its meaningful connections with past and future. The reference to song repeats his **allusion** to *The Birth of Tragedy*.

The Second Dance Song

In this second song to Life, Zarathustra implies that he has won dominion over that goddess. He recalls the advice of the old woman (in Of Old and Young Women), that women should be approached "with a whip." He has brought his whip, his strength and wisdom, to Life. At the conclusion, twelve strokes of a bell invoke the spirit of eternity. It is now midnight.

The Seven Seals

Zarathustra sings of his love for Eternity. All his wanderings have been for the sake of "eternal recurrence," for Eternity itself. His "wedding" with this spirit holds out the hope for children of his own creation. Such a child is Zarathustra himself, created and recreated, eternally. With this intense and lyrical affirmation of Zarathustra's desire for a union of the ideal man (himself) with the eternal, the third part of the book closes.

THUS SPOKE ZARATHUSTRA

TEXTUAL ANALYSIS

PART 4

The Honey Offering

The years pass by, and Zarathustra does not stir from his self-imposed loneliness. He sits upon the mountain peak, gazing into a dark landscape. His animals concerned for his welfare, ask if he is happy. He answers that he has too much happiness, that even his "happiness" oppresses him. His concern is for his work, not his happiness. He is like a ripe fruit; his veins are filled with honey. He decides, then, to climb a high mountain, telling the animals that he will offer "the honey offering."

When he reaches a high peak, he sends the animals away, so that he can meditate alone. By "the honey offering," he meant only a casting out of bait, to see what he can catch in the great sea of life. "Thus," he says, "men may now come up to me." He is merely waiting-for the day of his dominion.

Comment

The mood is somber and peaceful. The great, driving energy, which consumed him earlier, has fled. As the Prologue began by comparing Zarathustra to the sun, the fourth part begins by comparing him to a "ripe fruit." His "bestowing" has passed its active phase, and is now a passive virtue (see the Comment following The Dance Song). Others must now come to him; he will not seek them out. He is, he says, neither patient nor impatient, but "beyond" patience; for this is the nature of the "waiting" of a fruit on the tree.

A central **theme** of this section, and of the remainder of the book, is the question of the nature of happiness. Nietzsche rejects the moral theory of Utilitarianism (the theory of John Stuart Mill), which holds that the ultimate aim of all men is pleasure, and that "happiness" is made up of pleasures (this topic is also mentioned in the comment following Of the Thousand and One Goals). His work, Zarathustra says, is more important than his happiness; and the happiness he does have is oppressing, almost painful to him. Yet he is restless, and although he says he is not impatient, he is still "waiting." His present "happiness," then, may be contrasted with a further, different state, one which he will call "joy." The aim of man, according to Nietzsche, is the will to power, not self-preservation (Darwin) or pleasure (Mill). The internal feeling which comes with self-overcoming, realization of the meaning of eternal recurrence, and the consequent release of power, is "joy." Zarathustra will discuss this in The Intoxicated Song.

The Cry Of Distress

Now that Zarathustra has offered the "honey offering," visitors are not long in coming. The "prophet" appears before

Zarathustra (the prophet of nihilism). This prophet warns Zarathustra of coming disaster. Zarathustra, listening, hears a cry of distress. The prophet insists that it is the "Higher Man," crying out for Zarathustra. This thought horrifies Zarathustra, and he is seized by a feeling of apprehension and of anguish, but he rejects the prophet's suggestion that he should also feel pity. Then he takes heart, and chides the prophet, calling him a "morning raincloud." Having recovered his courage, he decides to seek out the source of the cry of distress. The prophet waits in the cave for Zarathustra's return.

Comment

Zarathustra, having completed his doctrine, is not certain of its outcome. This uncertainty can be a source of fear, but he has also the courage which he developed in his last overcoming: the courage to face nihilism, even if it seeks him out. Now, perhaps, Humanity seeks him out, and he is understandably concerned. Will his doctrine stand the test? Or will it be distorted? In any case, he is not inclined to turn back. This is to be the supreme test of his strength; he says that he has overcome his disgust for the weakness of man, but the prophet has frightened him with the prediction that he will succumb to the emotion of pity.

Conversation With The Kings

In the forest, Zarathustra comes across two Kings, in royal robes, driving a burdened ass before them. The Kings, conversing among themselves and not yet aware of Zarathustra's presence, reveal that they have fled their kingdoms because they are disgusted with the rabble, and because they no longer command respect. Tired of pretense and deception, they are traveling to seek the Higher Man, and his prophet, Zarathustra. Revealing himself, Zarathustra admits that he, too, seeks the Higher Man. He invites the Kings to his cave, and proceeds on his journey, for he has not yet found the source of the cry of distress.

Comment

The wandering Kings are a sign of the unsettled state of society, in which no real leaders are recognized, and in which there is a growing confusion of moralities. As Zarathustra had anticipated, his own doctrine is becoming of interest to men who, once powerful, have now lost their function. The presence of the Kings is also a comment on the uselessness of worldly power, which Nietzsche rejects in favor of the power which comes to the Self through sublimation. The ass represents those philosophers who formulate their systems in order to support the views of the powerful. In Of the Famous Philosophers, Zarathustra has said, of these philosophers, that "they always, as asses, pull - the people's cart!"

The Leech

As Zarathustra continues through the forest, he reaches a swamp. There, he accidentally steps upon a man, who is lying across the path. Frightened, and not realizing what it is that he has stumbled upon, Zarathustra strikes the man with his staff. When he sees that it is a man, however, he apologizes with a parable about a dog and a traveler, the point of which is that mistaken anger can drive apart those who may need each other most.

The man rises from his position, and in so doing he reveals that his arm is covered with blood. He explains that he has been studying leeches; in fact, his only study is the study of the brains of leeches. He is, he explains, the conscientious man of the spirit, who would rather know one thing well, than have a half-knowledge of many things. He is overjoyed, however, when he discovers that his companion is Zarathustra, for he has, in fact, been seeking him. He calls Zarathustra "the great leech of the conscience." He has been fascinated by Zarathustra's saying that "spirit is the life that itself cuts into life," evidently because this describes leeches, in a way, and also because it is apparently a description of the conscientious man's own method and way of life: "severe, stern, strict, cruel, inexorable."

Zarathustra, with some sarcasm, but not without friendliness, invites the stranger to his cave. But he himself continues his forest search.

Comment

Zarathustra's apology is an indication that he has, perhaps, been too harsh with the various pretenders to the Superman, whom he has previously criticized (see, for example, Of the Sublime Men). It is also clear that the Kings and the Conscientious Man have been impressed by various aspects of Zarathustra's teaching, but do not fully understand them. The Conscientious Man resembles the "inverse cripples" who have developed one faculty to the exclusion of all others (see Of Redemption). He has an overdeveloped conscience, which demands absolute honesty, and which is a burden to him. This is revealed by his reference to Zarathustra as "the leech of conscience." Conscience, itself, may be a drain upon one's energies; in which case the Conscientious Man may look upon Zarathustra as the very embodiment of the "will to truth," and therefore a symbol of this leech-like force. On the other hand, he may look to Zarathustra as a redeemer, who will drain his overworked conscience of its sting. This man restricts his study to the brain of the leech; this is a reference to Of Self-overcoming, in which Zarathustra pointed out that the study of the living creature in its "greatest and smallest paths" reveals the presence of the will to power. The Conscientious Man represents the Scientific Spirit as well, and Nietzsche thinks of Science as the greatest aid in the search for an earthly system of values.

The Sorcerer

Now Zarathustra comes upon an old man, who is in a state of great agitation, and who appears to be nearly overcome by a sense of isolation. Suddenly the old man breaks into a long poem, in which he bemoans his relation to an "unknown God" who has tormented him and made him prisoner, and then left him alone. Zarathustra, however, sees through the old man's ruse, and stops him with a blow from his staff. The old man admits that he was only singing as a jest, to bait Zarathustra into pity. He identifies himself as a "penitent of the spirit," but Zarathustra calls him an "actor who has lost faith in himself. The man agrees, admitting that he is not a great man, and that he seeks a truly great man for guidance. Zarathustra praises his honest confession, but says that he, himself, has "never yet seen a great man." He sends the sorcerer along to his cave, and proceeds even deeper into the forest.

Comment

This "Sorcerer" has been interpreted as a representation of the composer, Richard Wagner. However, the identification of the Sorcerer is a complex matter. He represents the creative artist, who must eventually feel the weight of his solitude, see his own baseness all too closely, and eventually come to struggle against himself "in caves and forests" - all of which has been described in Of the Way of the Creator. He also represents those who have turned aside from Zarathustra's teachings and have become pious (see Of the Apostates). Finally, the Sorcerer represents the "great man" in Of the Flies of the Market Place, whom Zarathustra also refers to as "the actor," whose faith shifts as the will of the people shifts, and whose belief in himself depends upon the number of people who believe in him. Nietzsche's discussion of Richard Wagner in his later book, *The Genealogy of Morals*, is a concise statement of these very points. Not only, then, is the sorcerer representative of Richard Wagner; Wagner, for Nietzsche, is a representative of the creative mentality which has entered a nihilistic phase, turned against itself, and is obsessed by loneliness. It is this phenomenon, not the man Wagner, which occupies Netzsche here.

Retired From Service

Zarathustra encounters another traveler; this is "the Last Pope," who has "retired from service" after learning of the death of God. He has wandered into the forest in search of a hermit, a pious old saint, of whom he has heard. But he has discovered that the hermit, too, is dead, and so now he seeks Zarathustra, the most pious of the Godless. Zarathustra takes the man's hand, and reveals his identity. The two men speak, for a while, of the death of God, which they agree was the result of excessive pity. God is accused of secrecy, of love tainted by the desire to judge (to mete out reward and punishment), of unclarity, and of many failures. Zarathustra, invoking his own love of honesty, says that it is better to have no God at all, than such a dishonest one. The "pope" replies that Zarathustra, in carrying honesty to such an extreme, is indeed a pious man. There is holiness in Zarathustra the "Godless." He asks to be Zarathustra's guest for the night, and Zarathustra directs him to the cave.

Comment

This passage associates piety and holiness with honesty and benediction, implying that Godlessness does not rule out these important religious values. The old hermit, now said to have passed away, is the very one who gave Zarathustra a friendly warning in the Prologue, and who had not yet heard of Zarathustra's message that "God is dead." The passage repeats the thought that the Christian value of honesty and truth eventually brings about the destruction of the Christian God himself, when it is found that there is no scientific basis for belief in His existence.

The Ugliest Man

Zarathustra enters a deserted valley of dark cliffs and no vegetation. Shepherds call this valley "serpent's death." Here he comes across the Ugliest Man, who has a riddle for Zarathustra. He asks, "What is the revenge on the witness?" Zarathustra is overwhelmed, momentarily, by pity for the creature, for its misery seems very great. Then he answers the riddle in a stern voice: the revenge on the witness is the murder of God. Man, who could not bear to be watched and known so well, has done away with God out of shame and desire for revenge against the witness and judge of that shame. The two men discuss pity, repeating the **theme** of the discourse Of the Compassionate, that pity is not a virtue and not a "modesty," but only stimulates a desire for revenge in the pitied. Zarathustra invites this stranger, as well, to his cave.

Comment

It has been suggested that the "Ugliest Man" represents the atheist. This, however, does not seem to be an adequate view. It is the people, themselves, who have murdered God. The Ugliest Man represents the ugliest thing in man, namely the Spirit of Revenge. In *The Genealogy of Morals* Nietzsche advances the view that primitive peoples invented God as a witness for their own inner punishment - the punishment of "bad conscience." But the morality of vengeance, associated with this God by Nietzsche (for as a witness, he is also a judge), eventually turns against its own creation and destroys it. In the previous section, it was suggested that God killed Himself, through pity. But Zarathustra there pointed out that the death of a God may have many causes: "When Gods die, they always die many kinds of death." This, then, is a third interpretation of the death of God; an overdeveloped sense of truth, excessive pity, and the Spirit of Revenge-all of these have been invoked as the cause. (See also *Beyond Good and Evil*, section 55.)

The Voluntary Beggar

Zarathustra is chilled, but suddenly he comes to an area of warmth and cheer. There, he finds a good and quiet man, seated among a herd of cows. The man, who is identified as "the Voluntary Beggar," is impressed by the wisdom of the cows: to ruminate and to lie in the sun. He is a "man of plants and roots," who has learned to "slow down," and who denies the distinction between "poor" and "rich." Zarathustra invites the man to his cave.

Comment

This is an obvious reference to the passage Of the Sublime Men. There, Zarathustra urged the "penitent of the spirit" to learn to lie down in the sunlight, to behave "like the ox," and to unlearn "contempt for the earth." It is his tension and violence of will that keeps him from becoming "exalted." The voluntary beggar represents that sense of harmony with nature which is most desirable in the men-to-come. He also represents, to a degree, Zarathustra himself, who has learned from hard experience, like the beggar, that it is "harder to give well than to take well."

The Shadow

As Zarathustra turns away, he hears yet another voice. It is the voice of his shadow, calling for him to wait. But Zarathustra is astounded by the number of people he has met in the forest, and begins to run away. He soon sees the folly of this, however, and stops. The Shadow, catching up, appears thin and worn. The Shadow complains that it has lost its way, and no longer has a sense of any goal. Zarathustra, however, warns the Shadow of the dangers of freedom. Freedom brings with it the desire to seize upon any security, however narrow or illusory. He directs the Shadow to his cave, where it may rest.

Comment

The Shadow represents Zarathustra's own freedom, which has been threatened by the presence of the visitors. Zarathustra has now met the last of the wanderers in his forest, and he still has not identified the source of the cry of distress. It is evident, however, that there will be quite a gathering at his cave: the two Kings, the Ass, the Conscientious Man, the Sorcerer, the "Last Pope," the Ugliest Man, the Voluntary Beggar, the Shadow, and the prophet; representatives of worldly power, philosophy, science, art, saintliness, revenge, ascetism, the guiding ideal, and nihilism. All of these are types of "Higher Men," once criticized by Zarathustra. The fact that he now welcomes them stems from his last overcoming, and his "convalescence," in which he reconciled himself with all the weaknesses of man. But there is more than meets the eye, in this gathering. More than once, the wanderers in the forest have been associated with "dogs"; and if not dogs, then with frogs (in the case of the Sorcerer) and cows. The two Kings state that they are fleeing from dogs, the Conscientious Man is likened to a dog in the parable, the Sorcerer compares himself to a dog in his song; the Last Pope, himself, hears the "howling of wild animals," and finds wolves in the old hermit's hut. And even the Ugliest Man says that he looks over "little people ... as a dog looks over ... sheep." There is no coincidence, certainly, in the fact that Nietzsche has constantly used "dogs" as a symbol of the repressed impulses, the "bad instincts," which need to be released and overcome by the Superman. In a deeper sense, then, these "Higher Men" represent elements of Zarathustra's own soul, elements which he, himself, has released after the transformation which occurred in The Convalescent. Zarathustra anticipated these events at that time, saying, "when the great man cries out," the pitiers, poets, "accusers of life," sinners, "bearers of the cross," and penitents "come running." The fact that he meets them all in a forest is also significant, since a forest is often a symbol, in folklore and mythology, of the realm of the "unconscious mind," the repository of repressed attitudes and feelings. And as before, the "prophet" appears, to serve as the catalyst for this development (see the Comment following Of Redemption). The subsequent material, then, may be seen as a stage in Zarathustra's own inner development, as well as a commentary on the "Higher Men."

At Noontide

Zarathustra, now alone in the forest, passes by an ancient tree, around which a coiled vine grows; from the vine hang ripe yellow grapes. The sun is directly overhead. It is noon. Zarathustra falls "asleep," but his eyes remain open. In this state of half-slumber, he speaks to himself. The world, it seems to him, has become "perfect." He feels a great happiness, a closeness to the earth, a fulfillment which cannot be accounted for. In the smallest things, he thinks, such as "the rustling of a lizard," lies the greatest happiness. He feels as if he has fallen into "the well of eternity," and yet he senses the beauty of the moment. The world is a "golden, round ring" in which "eternity" and "the moment" meet. Finally, with some difficulty, he arises, and departs with a question to the "well of eternity": "When will you drink my soul back into yourself?"

Comment

The tree is a transformation of the staff which was presented to Zarathustra by his disciples in Of the Bestowing Virtue. The vine is the serpent coiled about the staff, and the round, yellow grapes represent the sun at its top. The entirety is a symbol of Zarathustra's maturity, as well as his present condition of passive giving. All of the apprehension which was present when he first thought of entering the forest has left him, and his sense of fulfillment is the result of having released the "dogs in the cellar" and having come to no real harm. The closing passages are a reference to the doctrine of eternal recurrence. The man who has overcome himself is "redeemed," and the meaning given to each moment by the sense of its eternal recurrence becomes clear to him. Here, indeed, is a mystical sense of oneness with all things, anticipated in detail in The Seven Seals. There, the "wedding ring of rings," or the "Ring of Recurrence," is mentioned. Now, Zarathustra has completed the "marriage" with eternity which he longed for.

The Greeting

Zarathustra returns to his cave, and is startled to hear the cry of distress coming from within the cave itself. Inside, he discovers all of his "guests," and realizes that the cry came from them. They, together, are the Higher Man. He welcomes them, commenting on their melancholy spirit and the need for laughter. One of the Kings replies that the guests appreciate Zarathustra's humility, which is so coupled with pride that it does not lead them to disrespect, and that they are already losing their melancholy. Zarathustra's pride (the eagle has proved to be an uplifting influence. The King compares Zarathustra to a pine tree, reaching deep and growing high. Many despairing men, he says, are seeking this tree, this Zarathustra, and the solitude of Zarathustra has been broken. Those who seek him, says the king, are "the last remnant of God among men," who seek their last hope in Zarathustra.

Zarathustra now addresses the gathering. He is not inclined to accept these men as allies. They are still lacking in strength, and they are capable of distorting his teaching. The "evil dwarf" of nihilism is still with them, as well as the follies of the rabble. Zarathustra makes it clear that he looks upon these "Higher Men" as bridges only and not as ideals. They are stepping stones to the ideal man, but they are not a pattern for him. Zarathustra still awaits his own "children."

The Last Supper

The prophet interrupts the proceedings with a demand for wine and food. The Voluntary Beggar objects to the idea of an elaborate meal, for he dislikes gluttony. They do decide to eat, however, and the meal begins, which Zarathustra calls "the Last Supper."

Of The Higher Man

1-5. Zarathustra begins a recounting of his travels and his teachings. Now that God is dead, the "Higher Men" face their responsibility: that of serving as a bridge to the Superman. Zarathustra does not wish to preserve man, but to overcome him. The Higher Men have a source of strength which gives them some claim to superiority: they reject "petty prudence" (the moderate way expounded in Of the Virtue That Makes Small). He urges them to reject the doctrine that goodness lies in the "happiness of the greatest number." Courage, pride, and mastery of fear are the virtues which are worthy of praise. Anything which runs counter to the mediocrity of current morals is of some value. Even evil, then, is a strength, because it is a sign of freedom from this mediocrity (however, Zarathustra warns that his words here are "subtle"; he is not advocating "evil" in the ordinary sense of the term).

Comment

This is a further step in the rejection of "happiness" as the ultimate aim of human action. Zarathustra's view of "evil" here may best be interpreted in connection with passages such as Of the Three Evil Things, in which sensual pleasure, power, and selfishness are analyzed as "good" for the man who has overcome himself.

6-10. The Higher Men, however, do not measure up to the Superman, because they have not yet suffered through the disgust and subsequent reconciliation with man which Zarathustra has undergone. Zarathustra indicates that he does not look upon himself as an ideal, but rather as a necessary "shock," a catalyst, which will urge forward the process of evolution toward the Superman. He is wary of "ideals," because they can be turned too readily into "afterworlds." A healthy mistrust and a firm honesty, then, are desirable qualities. Those who attempt to exalt rigid, fixed patterns - the "learned" - are especially to be watched. There is no ultimate truth: "He who cannot lie does not know what truth is." No "ideal" can help man; he has to pull himself upward alone, and with the courage which can face a future in which any predetermined goal is absent.

Comment

The notion of a connection between falsehood and truth will be discussed at greater length in the first part of *Beyond Good and Evil*. Nietzsche looks upon science, itself, as a kind of "falsehood." This is a necessary consequence of his firm conviction that there is no ultimate truth. But Nietzsche, however, affirms such "falsehood," and does not find grounds for pessimism in it.

11-15. Creative spirits must be able to bear solitude, without fleeing into "piety" (see The Sorcerer). The nature of true creativity demands that action should not be for the sake of others, but only for the self. This, however, is the "selfishness" of the pregnant woman, who must care for herself in order to produce the child. Such a selfishness, furthermore, is not a seeking for pleasure: "One does not give birth for pleasure." The solitary artist must necessarily create from his own resources, and nothing will emerge from his solitude that has not come from what he, himself, has taken into it. If the creative spirit fails, this is not the greatest disaster. There are, after all, many small perfections in the world, many beauties, many accomplishments. These must not be overlooked. "Perfect things teach hope".

Comment

A further reference to the subordinate position of the "pleasure principle" of Utilitarianism, and a preparation for the later discussion of "joy." Nietzsche has already said that the creative process is the most valuable thing (see Of the Thousand and One Goals). If pleasure is not a part of its essence, then the doctrine that pleasure is the source of happiness and the standard of value must be false.

16-20. Zarathustra eulogizes laughter, the great remedy for failure. He condemns the "uncompromising man" who rejects laughter. Nothing, he says, can follow a perfectly straight path. We stumble, we fall, we even "stand on our heads" - and laughter is the balm which makes light of our wounds. Therefore Zarathustra christens himself "the laughing prophet." Laughter, too, is an antidote for that affliction produced by the Spirit of Gravity: the "heavy feet" of nihilism and pessimism. Laughter is, in fact, a companion of freedom, and the soul that can laugh can also "dance to its own pipe."

SUMMARY

> Nietzsche rejects the pursuit of mediocrity and "general happiness." He denies that man should govern his actions by externally imposed, fixed ideals, and he warns against absolute "truth" and even against Zarathustra, taken as a fixed ideal. Creative souls, especially, must not merge themselves with the crowd, but accept the burden of "creative selfishness," and learn to bear the solitude which accompanies it. Failure, which is, perhaps, inevitable, is not disaster. Little perfections and laughter are bulwarks against nihilism.

The Song Of Melancholy

Zarathustra steps out of his cave, leaving the gathering of "Higher Men" at the table. No sooner is he gone, however, than the sorcerer (who has already shown his cunning by trying to seduce Zarathustra into pity) springs from his seat, and begins a song of melancholy, in which he bemoans the poet's inability to attain truth. He distorts Zarathustra's teaching by placing the images of the cat (that is, the "lion" which represents courage) and the eagle (pride) in a context of frustration. Courage, pride, even laughter, are doomed in the end, because the poet can never attain "truth," and therefore is, in the last analysis, a fool.

Of Science

Only the Conscientious Man resists the Sorcerer's cunning distortion of Zarathustra's doctrine. He takes away the Sorcerer's harp, and cries out for Zarathustra. Even in attacking the Sorcerer, however, this man of science reveals his own infirmity, for he reveals that he looks upon Zarathustra as a symbol of the security which science seeks. Fear, he says, motivates science, especially fear of the irrational side of man. Zarathustra has entered the cave and heard this speech, and he corrects the Conscientious Man. Fear is not the fundamental attribute of man, but rather courage. Then a jest causes them all to laugh, and the tension abates.

Comment

The rejection of the Conscientious Man's view that fear is the basis of all human striving represents a further denial of the principle of the "survival of the fittest." Nietzsche does not believe that self-preservation is the dominant human drive. It is, rather, the will to power, and the chief virtue of this will is courage. The Conscientious Man, on the basis of this passage, may be thought of as representing the scientist Darwin.

Among The Daughters Of The Desert

Zarathustra is about to leave the cave again, but his shadow urges him to stay. The shadow is afraid of the somber mood which still lingers after the sorcerer's song. He takes the harp, and sings his own song of oriental sensuality and of the clear air of the desert. The song is overlaid with the message that Western man cannot fully deny his moral heritage, and he carries the seeds of "virtuous dignity" even into the desert (it is thus a repetition of Zarathustra's earlier comment that a man finds, in his solitude, only what he himself brings to it).

The Awakening

The song, however, cheers up the company, and Zarathustra slips out once again. He feels that the "Higher Men" have won out over the Spirit of Gravity; their laughter has dispelled nihilism. He interprets this as a sign that they are overcoming their disgust, even as he has done. They are now "convalescents" (see The Convalescent).

But Zarathustra's pleasure in this development is short-lived. A sudden silence within the cave draws him back, and there he observes a grotesque scene: all of the men are praying, and the object of their worship is the Ass. The Ugliest Man, after some difficulty, intones a lengthy "litany" in praise of this animal, and every so often the Ass affirms the point by uttering "Ye-a." The substance of the ugliest man's speech, however, is a sarcastic criticism of philosophers that repeats the material given in Of the Great Philosophers.

The Ass Festival

Zarathustra is horrified by this turn of events, and he demands an explanation. The "Last Pope" explains that the Ugliest Man has brought God back to life in the form of the ass, because it is better to worship anything rather than nothing at all (he appears to reject Zarathustra's view that it is better to have no God at all than a bad one, which he had praised, in a way, in Retired from Service). Zarathustra asks the Ugliest Man for an account of his behavior, but he receives only a joking answer. Zarathustra now realizes that the "ritual" was a jest. Yet he makes a point of it: the "Higher Men" are indeed convalescents, and they look to a festival, even an "Ass Festival," to warm their souls, even as Zarathustra had taken pleasure in music after his own convalescence.

Comment

The intent of the passage is that one may find a certain solace, and even a sense of perspective, in philosophy, but that it must not be taken too seriously. The ability to look upon such things lightly is the best sign of a healthy spirit.

The Intoxicated Song

The final **climax** of the book has been reached. The company steps out into the night air, and even the ugliest man affirms his love of the earth. Zarathustra, seeing the Higher Men in a state of recovery, is again overtaken by a feeling of union with eternity, A bell tolls midnight. As the strokes ring out, Zarathustra speaks of his great joy, a joy beyond mere pleasure. Each statement is followed by a line from the poem to eternity from The Second Dance Song. All time, now, has become one: "midnight is also noonday." The joy of the Superman is a painful joy, for the affirmation of one part of existence requires the affirmation of all existence, and this includes suffering and woe. It is this realization which came over Zarathustra in The Convalescent, and now he affirms it in the full presence of his nihilistic tendencies (represented by the gathering of Higher Men). He has not succumbed to them; he has overcome them.

Comment

In this way, the doctrine of eternal recurrence is restated. Nietzsche has added a corollary: every event, even the most minute, is a part of the greater whole of existence. He who seeks true happiness in the moment must find it in eternity as well. This is why joy is painful. All of the woe in the world must be accepted before any real union of the moment with eternity can occur. The mystical experience of any deep meaning in life, then, is necessarily also a tragic one. Joy and pain are not contrary to one another, and the Utilitarian view that man seeks pleasure and avoids pain is rejected. This **theme** is also treated in Nietzsche's last book, *The Will to Power* (no. 699), and in *The Birth of Tragedy* (see the section in this outline titled Beauty in Art).

The Sign

On the following morning, Zarathustra awakens before the sleeping Higher Men. He is again like the sun; his passive stage is over. He understands fully, now, that the Higher Men are not his own "children," not the men-to-come. Suddenly, a flock of doves surrounds him, and a great lion appears before him. The lion rests at his feet and licks his hands affectionately. He takes this as a sign that the children of his "wedding" with eternity are soon to come. The Higher Men are now awake, and they begin to emerge from the cave. But the lion, with a tremendous roar, frightens them away. Zarathustra has not been seduced by the appeal to pity which they represented, and his last test is complete.

Comment

The lion represents Zarathustra's overcoming of his own nihilistic tendencies. It also is an indication that he has reached a higher level of creative ability than his affirmative, vigorous state of mind at the beginning of part two. A natural implication of the appearance of the lion, is that the process of self-development and creativity is never-ending, and that it moves upward through successive repetitions of the three stages of the soul given in Of the Three Metamorphoses. It is, then, an expression of Nietzsche's view that man must overcome himself again and again. Zarathustra, however, has felt true joy, and has been given a sign of even greater things to come. On this optimistic and happy note, the book is concluded.

BEYOND GOOD AND EVIL

TEXTUAL ANALYSIS

PART 1

....

INTRODUCTION

Beyond Good and Evil was written in 1885, immediately after *Thus Spoke Zarathustra*. Nietzsche conceived of it as a detailed and refined criticism of contemporary life. As such, it reflects and amplifies many of the chapters of Zarathustra in which society, politics, philosophy, art, and science are held up to the measure of the Superman, and found wanting. It was Nietzsche's profound conviction that the moral interpretation of the world, which he attacked with great acidity in *Zarathustra*, has entered into every phase of modern thought, with unfortunate and even disastrous effect. His hope is to "pry loose" the courageous thinker from this clinging "prejudice." His style, therefore, is vigorous, witty, touched with sarcasm, and often violent. He sometimes takes countermeasures which are so extreme that they do not truly represent his own final views; the intent is, rather, to shock the reader into reconsidering opinions which may have been taken for granted. The book is constructed of short, aphoristic passages, and there is not always a clear connection between them. This aphoristic construction reaches a peak in chapter four, "Apothegms and Interludes," where each aphorism is a sentence or two in length. Since it is hardly possible to distill further that in which a maximum of purity has been reached, this chapter, a short one, is not treated here. The reader who has read and understood the remainder of the commentary, however, should have little difficulty in rooting out the meaning of the separate epigrams.

The title, *Beyond Good and Evil*, expresses the general **theme**: what results when the moral interpretation of the world is rejected? In part three of *Thus Spoke Zarathustra*, the following passage may be found: "Almost in the cradle are we presented with heavy words and values: this dowry calls itself 'Good' and 'Evil.' For its sake we are forgiven for being alive." These words, which occur in the section titled Of the Spirit of Gravity, express, Nietzsche's conviction that the moral interpretation of the world is like a weight fastened about man, dragging him down into the abyss of nihilism - the conviction that life is absurd. *Beyond Good and Evil* is an investigation of the ways in which this burden manifests itself, and an attempt to explain the nature of the "free spirit" - man unfettered by the chains of morality.

It would be a great misunderstanding, however, to assume that Nietzsche advocates a life based upon impulse, arbitrary decision, and lack of responsibility. His own ideal, Zarathustra, is a man who struggles for self-control, love of mankind, and an overflow of benevolence. But Zarathustra must do this without the "crutch" afforded by a moral interpretation of things, and in the fact of that abiding nihilism which threatens at every turn to destroy those who attempt to walk free. Man must learn to live well without belief in an afterlife, in "absolutes," in black-and-white contrasts. To do this, he must know himself, affirm himself, and overcome self-disgust. Only then will he extend his spirit "beyond good and evil."

Preface

Nietzsche introduces several leading ideas: (1) There is no absolute truth; (2) Dogmatism in philosophy is coming to an end; (3) Certain "dogmas," however, are still entrenched in our language, and therefore a part of our thought (for example, belief in an immortal soul); (4) The greatest, and worst, dogmatic view was Plato's theory that there existed an Absolute Good and a "Pure Spirit"; (5) The essence of life is seeing things in perspective, and therefore the dogmatism of the Absolute goes contrary to the essence of life (since an "absolute" truth is one which holds good from all points of view, and therefore does not admit perspective); (6) The present state of European culture (1885) is one of tension, resulting from the downfall of dogmatism; (7) Neither an intensified religious feeling (Jesuitism) nor "Democracy" have released this tension; (8) There may be "Free Spirits" who have the ability to provide the needed redirection of social distress.

1 Prejudices Of Philosophers

1. The desire to obtain absolute truths, which Nietzsche calls "the will to truth," eventually leads man to ask about the nature of truth itself. An even more basic and dangerous question is the following: what is the value of truth?

2. Philosophers, at least those who may be called "metaphysicians, have been possessed by a fundamental, but erroneous, assumption: "the belief in antitheses of values."

Comment

This "prejudice" is, basically, the belief that anything which is unqualifiedly good must have an opposite, which is unqualifiedly bad. This belief includes the corollary that an impurity of the "good," any mingling of it with the "bad," corrupts and defiles it. This prejudice regarding the application of the terms "good" and "bad" has its **metaphysical** correlate (i.e., a related view about the nature of existence) in the view that there exist, in nature, sets of opposites. These opposites are sometimes referred to as opposed "realms of Being." Examples are truth/error; objectivity/personal interest; the thing-in-itself/the world of "phenomena"; form/matter; "universals"/"individuals"; spirit/flesh; mind/body; the stable/the unstable; the theoretical/the practical. In general, philosophers (and societies) have attached a positive value, "good," to the first members of these pairs, and a negative value, "bad," to their opposites. (Nietzsche does not give all of these examples at this point.)

Connected with these two aspects (the moral and the **metaphysical**) of this prejudice is the belief that nothing can emerge from its opposite. Truth, for example, can never arise out of error, and Spirit can never emerge from mere Flesh. This philosophical "prejudice of opposites," then, may be divided into three parts:

1. Whatever is good-without-qualification has, as its opposite, the bad-without-qualification (and vice versa).

2. There are kinds of existence (e.g., "Spirit") which are entirely separate from an opposite kind of existence (e.g., "Flesh").

3. Nothing ever arises out of its opposite.

Nietzsche attacks this threefold assumption, as an application of his principle that dogmatism is at an end. He suggests:

1. Perhaps such antitheses simply do not exist.

2. Even if they do exist, perhaps they are not absolutes, but are dependent upon one another:

    a. The values assigned to them may be valid only from a certain point of view;

    b. The value of one member of a pair may be derived from its relationship to the "opposite" member;

    c. It is even possible that there are so-called "opposites" which are essentially identical, and that the value of one part lies in its basic identity with the opposite part (for example, "illusion" and "reality" may be, fundamentally, manifestations of the same thing-a view similar to that of the English philosopher Berkeley).

Nietzsche expresses his belief that philosophers are now developing in whom this prejudice will be overcome, and who will dare to investigate the alternatives he has suggested.

Comment

Historically speaking, Nietzsche's account of the philosophical prejudice in favor of "opposites" goes back to the ancient Greek philosophers. Parmenides (ca. 510 B.C.) placed the highest reality (and the highest value) in stability, while his counterpart Heraclitus (ca. 500 B.C.) insisted that the world was in a constant state of change. It should be noted that philosophical monism (the belief that all reality is the manifestation of a single element, such as Spirit) is not necessarily free from the "prejudice of opposites." The monist usually has accepted a set of opposites, but simply denied the existence of one in favor of the other.

In modern times, philosophical pragmatism follows Nietzsche's hypothesis by denying absolute "dualisms" (represented by the sets of opposites) and asserting a continuity among all parts of nature. The American philosopher John Dewey, for example, feels that the value of theoretical activity (and thought in general) lies only in its intimate connection with practice and with practical matters. Nietzsche himself expresses his opposition to such dualisms, for example, in his book *The Genealogy of Morals*, in which he links psychological (i.e., mental) distress to physiological (i.e., physical) troubles, such as bad diet and disease.

3. Nietzsche attacks the view that conscious thought is opposed to instinctive behavior. Even the most well-thought-out and apparently objective logical conclusions of philosophers are, perhaps, heavily influenced by the instincts of the thinker. The subjective valuations of the philosopher, which may be fundamentally a matter of heredity or an expression of physiological needs, enter into his thought and direct its course.

Comment

The American philosopher William James has expressed this thought in classic form. He felt that the philosophical system supported by a given philosopher is largely a reflection of that philosopher's temperament. Philosophers are either "tender-minded" or "tough-minded," and their philosophical views tend to reflect their psychological disposition. There may also be a difference in the temper of social groups. When the degree of control of the changing aspects of the environment is low, or when wealth and food are scarce, the belief in an ideal spiritual realm may be more attractive than it would be, say, in a time of scientific achievement and bountiful crops. (William James (1842-1910) was a contemporary of Nietzsche.)

4. Nietzsche introduces a thesis which fully expresses his dissatisfaction with the traditional interpretation of "opposite." He suggests that falsehood may be more valuable than truth. The test of value may be the usefulness of a thing (or belief), rather than its objectivity. Certain fundamental beliefs are nothing more than convenient "fictions." For example, propositions which many philosophers have taken to be necessarily true, such as the "synthetic a priori" propositions that "every event has a cause" and "all colored objects have some spatial extent," are not objectively founded. They are universally accepted only because they are "indispensable." Nietzsche calls these propositions "logical fictions." Such "untruth," he says, is a "condition of life."

Comment

Nietzsche's use of the word "logical" here is not clear, but many modern philosophers have suggested that the apparently necessary truth of such propositions is a result of the structure of language. As such, these may be called "logically true" propositions, in a loose sense of the word "logical." Since they are not absolutes, but depend upon the structure of language, they may be termed fictions. But it is clear that Nietzsche is not using the terms "fiction" and "untruth" in the ordinary sense of these words. At the least, he means simply nonabsolute truths (but if "truth" is thought of as something that must be absolute, then this expression is a contradiction in terms). What Nietzsche denies here is that there is any absolute truth or absolute error; instead, there are more or less valuable beliefs. If what is valuable changes, these beliefs may change. They are, therefore "untruths" in the strict sense.

5-8. Nietzsche repeats the view that systems held by philosophers are expressions of temperament. There is, he says, a certain hypocrisy in philosophers who fail to admit this, and who insist that their views are dictated by pure reasoning. This element of hypocrisy has led people to look upon them with a degree of distrust. Kant and Spinoza, he says, are good examples.

In accordance with this general thesis, Nietzsche denies that the desire for knowledge is the basic motivation for philosophy. Instead, he is inclined to analyze the systems of famous philosophers in terms of their moral valuations. Any philosopher who might turn out to be truly concerned with knowledge and objectivity is probably not primarily a philosopher; his true inclinations must have some other outlet. A true philosopher always reflects his "deepest impulses" in his thought. Philosophers, in a sense, are "actors." They are also like the beast of burden, the ass.

Comment

The general **theme** of these sections is expressed many times in *Thus Spoke Zarathustra*. The use of the term "actors" in such a context occurs in Of the Flies of the Market Place (in part one of that book); the ass, also, becomes a symbol for philosophers who carry "the people's cart" (the traditional morality), in Of the Famous Philosophers, and in part four (The Conversation with the Kings and The Awakening).

9. Nietzsche disagrees with philosophers who urge a return to "nature" (as the Greek Stoics, whose supreme rule was sequi naturam, to "follow nature"). The term "nature," he points out, may have two meanings: the universe independent of the intrusion of human efforts, or the universe inclusive of men and their purposes. If the first is meant, then the rule "follow nature" is impossible to follow, for nature, in this sense, is everything that man cannot dare to be: boundless, purposeless, immoral, and irrational-in short, indifferent and unlimited. Man cannot exist without imposing boundaries, justice, and reason upon things. Virtue, for man, is just the opposite of nature, in this sense of the term. But in the second sense, the rule is meaningless, since man cannot do otherwise than "live according to life."

Nietzsche sees a hidden motive in the Stoic doctrine. He feels that those who hold to a rule of this sort want to interpret nature in accordance with their own values, and then, apparently "finding" these values in nature, they insist that all men should follow them. This is, of course, erroneous, and is a special case of the construction of a metaphysics (theory of existence) that suits the values and temperament of the philosopher.

10. The interest of philosophers in the problem of the "real and the apparent world" ("opposites" whose relation to one another constitutes the "problem") is partly due to the "will to truth." For the most part, however, it is the result of a desire to return to the past. Philosophers who reject the apparent world and who may even doubt the existence of their own bodies (such as Descartes) may be seeking to return to the security of the older belief in the "immortal soul." This may be a sign of

"good taste," since present-day philosophy is too scattered and indiscriminate to offer a desirable alternative.

11. The philosopher Immanuel Kant (1724-1804) answered his most difficult question by a logical "trick." When considering the question, "How are synthetic judgments a priori possible?", he answered by proposing the existence of a "faculty" which makes such judgments possible. This, says Nietzsche, is no real explanation at all, but merely begs the question. It is the same as explaining the sleep-inducing properties of opium by appealing to a "power" of producing sleep (it produces sleep because it has a power to produce sleep).

Comment

"Synthetic judgments a priori" are judgments that appear to be necessarily true (true in all possible circumstances), whose truth does not require any experimental verification, but which "convey information" about the world in a way that definitions, for example, do not. Examples have been given in section 4 above. The English philosopher David Hume (1711-1776) had claimed that all propositions which convey information were only probable, but never absolutely certain. Kant held that this was not so.

Nietzsche criticizes German philosophers for falling into this logical blunder, and using Kant as a justification for the invention of even more spurious "faculties." He repeats his view (in section 4) that the belief in "synthetic judgments a priori" is a false one, but a useful one which is necessary for the support of a certain (human) perspective. He does not, however, explain the nature of this "necessity" or the needs which it satisfies.

12. Nietzsche expresses his approval of the discrediting of the theory of materialistic atomism (the theory, stemming from the Greek Democritus, that everything is made up of indivisible and irreducible units of matter). But the tendency to postulate the existence of such ultimate indivisibles may still be an influence in maintaining the belief in a "soul-atom" - an indestructible, indivisible spiritual unit considered to be the source of all mental and emotional life. This influence should be rejected. Our view of the "soul" needs to be refined. Modern psychology should consider the soul as the result of an alteration of instincts by social structures (and as such, changeable).

13. The instinct of "self-preservation" is not the basic instinct of man. The most fundamental instinct, according to Nietzsche, is the will to power. Psychology should construct theories accordingly.

14. Natural philosophy (the natural sciences) does not provide an explanation of the world; it only describes it, and to an extent arranges it to suit our purposes. Being based upon a belief in the senses, however, it is readily taken to be an explanation (namely, a materialistic one). It also differs from Platonism, which rejects the world of the senses as a means to truth, and in this opposition to Platonism, natural philosophy is like a philosophic explanation of things. Platonism is a more refined, aristocratic view, but the scientific outlook has its practical value.

15. The belief in the reality of the world which is perceived by the senses, which natural science must take for granted, is not easily rejected. If it is held that we do not perceive the world as it really is, because our sense organs distort the impressions which we receive, it may be argued in return that our belief in

the existence and nature of these very sense organs is derived from sense experience; the theory, therefore, is self-defeating.

16. In addition to the synthetic judgments a priori (see sections 4 and 11 above), which are always general in nature, there are certain other propositions which philosophers have held to be absolutely certain. These are the so-called "immediate certainties," such as the proposition "I think." Such propositions, are commonly supposed to be known by an act of perception, rather than by an intellectual process. Nietzsche denies that such propositions can be known to be certain in this way. The very expression "immediate certainty" seems to him to be a self-contradiction (he does not, however, support this view).

An analysis of "I think" reveals that it depends upon a number of assumptions which are not self-evident at all; something is happening, but in order to identify it as thinking, we must (1) know what thinking is, (2) determine whether or not the present occurrence is thinking (which involves comparison and is not immediate), (3) determine whether or not there must be a thing which does the thinking, and (4) identify this thing, if any, with "I." These things cannot be determined by a direct perception.

Comment

Nietzsche refers to the thesis of the French philosopher Rene Descartes (1596-1650), that "I think" cannot be doubted, and whose "I think, therefore I am" ("Cogito, ergo sum") is famous. Nietzsche's basic weapon in this attack upon the "rationalist" view of Descartes is his conviction that the "ego" (or the "I") is a spurious entity, invested out of the necessity to provide a responsible agent for human acts. It is, then, a reflection of his denial of "soul-atomism" and his call for a new psychology of the soul in section 12. The next section is an elaboration of this theme.

17-19. The idea that thought requires a subject, "I," which does the thinking, is one which derives from overattention to grammar. Since what happens in thinking is expressed by a sentence "I think," it is assumed that the word "think" refers to the action, and the word "I" refers to an agent which carries out the action. But this may be a **metaphysical** error, just as the "atoms" were introduced to play the part of the substance within which "qualities" reside, under the influence of the subject-predicate formula, e.g., "It is red." The belief in "free will" stems from a similar error - the free will is postulated as the "agent" of moral responsibility. Such theories may have retained their fascination simply because acute thinkers have found them challenging enough to use them as exercises.

Regarding this "free will," however: popular grammar makes it relatively easy to fall into the trap of looking upon the moral agent (the free will) as a simple, uncomplicated unit. Actually it is a very complex matter, and we should not be misled by grammatical simplicity. An act of "free will" involves, for example:

1. a complex of sensations;

2. the operation of a multitude of habits;

3. an act of rational thought, or a process of deliberation, which is not mere "will";

4. an emotion of "command";

5. a corresponding feeling of "obedience";

6. definite (but often overlooked) sensations of resistance (of habits, of muscles, of thought, of environment); and

7. an "elation" as a result of the feeling of power which ensues when the resistances are overcome.

In the presence of all these factors, it is folly to think that willing alone is sufficient for the carrying out of an action. Willing, as decision or wish, is only a part of a cooperative process, involving many parts of the soul (see the comment on the complexity of the soul in section 12). In fact, the complete human organism is a hierarchy of many "souls," and an act of will involves relations of command and obedience among these "souls." The study of morals is the study of the "relations of supremacy" among social groups; the study of the will, therefore, is included under the study of morals (Nietzsche has already suggested that the "soul" is a social function-section 12).

Comment

Nietzsche's view here bears a strong resemblance to that expressed in one of John Dewey's most influential books, Human Nature and Conduct (*Bright Notes?*). This book is guided primarily by the idea that habit and thought are not opposites (see section 3), but are functionally related. Dewey shares Nietzsche's view that there are no **metaphysical** "opposites," and that both habit and thought are conditioned by society.

20. Expanding upon his view that overattention to grammar may lead to philosophical error, sections 17-19, Nietzsche suggests that the grammar of an entire language may restrict and direct the philosophical thought undertaken by those who think and speak in it. From this it follows that philosophical

ideas, within a given linguistic-cultural unit of society, are not separate from one another, but closely interlinked; even the philosophical alternatives which present themselves may be limited by the common language structure. Finally, it is possible that the structure of a language is reducible to the presence of common valuations, which Nietzsche links, as usual, to physiological needs.

Comment

This idea, that valuations, language, and philosophies are all interdependent and related to common social conditions, reflects Nietzsche's view in *Thus Spoke Zarathustra* that the morality of a society may be inferred from its environmental conditions (see Of the Thousand and One Goals, in part one of that book). It has been anticipated here by the Comment in the Preface, where it is listed as item (3).

21. Nietzsche denies that there can be anything which is its own cause (causa sui). The doctrine of free will, however, is based upon an acceptance of this self-contradiction. What may frighten some thinkers into entertaining this folly, he suggests, is their fear that a caused will (a will affected by causes other than itself) is a "nonfree" will, and hence the admission of external causes would render freedom of will impossible. But this reasoning, Nietzsche insists, rests upon a mistaken idea of "cause." The cause does not force the effect; it is not a species of compulsion. This mistaken idea is the result of a "push and pull" doctrine of causality, which looks upon cause and effect in terms of the model of one thing pushing or pulling another, thereby compelling it to move. Actually, causality is just a part of the scientific organization of natural phenomena (see section 14). Cause and effect are "pure conceptions," and do not represent

any physical necessity. The "free will" is simply one which is relatively less obstructed by internal and external resistances (see section 19). Belief, or nonbelief, in freedom of the will is largely a reflection of the temperament of the individual.

22. The belief that causality is a relationship of necessity among events (that events are "compelled" to take place by causal action) is partly the result of a misunderstanding of the expression "law of nature."

Comment

The error lies in taking the word "law" in its prescriptive sense. In this sense, it refers to laws prescribed by social institutions and law courts. Those who violate prescriptive laws are subject to punishment. It is assumed, therefore, that "natural law" cannot be "violated" without some form of punishment. This "natural punishment" would be infallible, since nature itself is the judge and jury. Hence the often-held belief that natural law is only violable in special, "supernatural" cases, such as "miracles." But in fact a "law" of nature does not represent an edict laid down by some inviolable authority, but is merely a statistical representation of observed patterns-a descriptive law - and it does not carry any necessity with it. For further discussion of this issue, see John Hospers, Introduction to Philosophical Analysis, Chapter 4.

23. Psychology, too, has been influenced by "moral prejudices." The science of psychology must come to admit the important place in mental life of emotions and instincts which have been considered "bad." The splitting of all instincts into "good" ones and "bad" ones must be abandoned; research should be "beyond good and evil," abandoning the prejudice of

moral opposites. Such a free psychology will be the "queen of the sciences." (Compare this passage with Of the Tree on the Mountainside, from *Thus Spoke Zarathustra*, part one.)

Comment

The philosophical prejudices which Nietzsche has discussed in this first chapter may now be summarized:

1. The prejudice of opposites (section 2).

2. The tendency to introduce "faculties" as explanations (section 11).

3. The belief in absolute certainties, either intellectual (section 4) or intuitive (section 16).

4. The tendency to postulate the existence of "atom-like" entities as subjects in which qualities reside, or as agents for human actions (section 12).

5. The general tendency to be dominated and misled by grammar, supposing that the structure of the world must reflect the structure of grammar.

The last of these may be considered as primary. All the others are, in one way or another, manifestations of 5. If we go a step further, pointing out Nietzsche's thesis that "grammar" is in turn reducible to "valuations," then 1 through 4 above may be taken as an expression of the moral interpretations of the world; that is, they are **metaphysical** theories which are adopted because they conform to the values of the society.

BEYOND GOOD AND EVIL

TEXTUAL ANALYSIS

PART 2 - 5

2 The Free Spirit

24. Man has the tendency to simplify the world, in order to obtain a certain degree of freedom from particular circumstances. Language is the primary structure through which this "simplification" is achieved-especially in its tendency to emphasize "opposites" where, according to Nietzsche, there are only "degrees and refinements of gradation." This simplification is, in an absolute sense, a falsification. But it is necessary as a support for life.

Comment

The process of classification provides a simple example of this point. When we classify more than one animal as, say, "rabbit," we exhibit a tendency to falsify by ignoring individual differences in favor of certain useful similarities. Classification is, then, both a falsification and a valuation. There was a time when whales, for example, were classified as fish, until it became more useful to classify them as mammals. In both cases, the classification minimizes certain real relationships in favor of others: it simplifies. Similarly, it is useful to "lump together" actions such as willing, feeling, and thinking, under one heading, "mental," and to postulate a contrasting heading, "physical," for a different group of activities. In this way, "opposites" arise. But for a more refined scientific method, these classifications may have to be modified greatly.

25-26. Nietzsche warns philosophers not to become martyrs for the sake of "truth." He is especially concerned with agnostics who suspend all judgment until they are able to obtain certainty-which never comes. This long suspension of judgment can only lead to bad temper. Philosophers should seek out a "solitude" free from the prejudices represented by the "will to truth." Only when he is free should the philosopher dare to study man. Cynics, who criticize humanity from a cool, even-tempered point of view, but who never become free from man themselves, are nevertheless valuable guides, because they represent a certain degree of honesty. They are better, in this respect, than those who engage in violent self-condemnation. (See Of Passing By, in part three of *Thus Spoke Zarathustra*.)

27-29. The German language, as a reflection of racial, social, and physiological conditions, is not easily suited for the rapidity of thought necessary for a "free spirit." Nietzsche, who has (as a philologist) a certain freedom from this linguistic burden, often finds it difficult to express himself in German. Thought may be presto, lento, or staccato (rapid, slow, or choppy). German does not lend itself to thought which is presto. If the "free spirit," to move "beyond and evil," must transcend the natural rhythms of his language, he must therefore bear a certain degree of isolation from his fellows.

The free spirit is not only isolated, but he also has no place of refuge, since he can never return, entirely, to his original state. Further, he is beset by dangers. By attempting to overcome the simplifications which language introduces into things, he exposes himself to the uncertainties which this simplification serves to counteract. Since he cannot wholly deny his heritage, he is also subject to attacks of bad conscience and remorse.

30. Values depend upon one's point of view. The values that suit a "lower order of human beings" may not be useful at all for a "higher order." The perspectives from which a given mode of action may be weighed and valued are either exoteric (public) or esoteric (private). Certain beliefs and ideas, for example, may be extremely dangerous from a public point of view, but highly desirable from the point of view of the creative mentality. There is, in other words, a double standard of valuation.

31-33. The simplification of things into contrasting opposites which may be easily affirmed or denied, is a sign of youthful impetuosity. A more mature view, becoming at last aware of this oversimplification, must suffer through a period of self-distrust (when it is realized that what once seemed so clear and certain is not so, one's judgment itself is called into question).

Comment

The advent of self-appraisal and thence self-control was taken by Nietzsche to be the essence of morality. His reference here to the development of an individual is a prelude to the consideration of a similar social development.

In the earliest times, men judged the worth of an action by referring to its results. "Success" and "failure" determined the attitude one might take toward an action. This period may be called the pre-moral era. The moral era was introduced when the value of an action came to be referred to its origin. The origin of an action, however, was taken to be an intention (on the part of a "free will"). This was a step forward, because it produced a certain degree of control and reflection, and an assumption of habits of individual self-criticism and responsibility. However, it rests upon the erroneous assumption that the origin of an action is an intention. A further stage, which may be called ultra-moral, is introduced by taking the intention as a mere symptom of the true origin of the action, and seeking the origin in the more complex factors of the personality (factors which a "free" psychology may discover). The morality of intentions leads to a blank wall of self-renunciation; this morality must be reappraised. Thus Nietzsche distinguishes three stages of morality: pre-moral, moral, and ultramoral.

34-38. Just as the youth may come to mistrust his judgment when he discovers his mistakes, thinkers may come to distrust all rational thought when they discover that it is inherently falsification. The philosopher must abandon belief in "certainties" and assume a distrustful attitude. But this is not cause for regret; the value of "certainty" has been overestimated. What is really valuable is that perspective which works best. Even the idea that a perceiver, the "subject," provides a fixed point for knowledge, is questionable. The "subject" itself may be a fiction. The subject-predicate grammar misleads us here.

Both the subjective world and the objective world may be aspects of a single process - the action of will to power, represented by the complex, active interchange among organism and environment ("self-regulation, assimilation, nutrition, secretion, and change of matter"). The "objective world" is perhaps, simply a part of whatever enters into this process. But to say this is not to make the world "subjective," as the philosopher Berkeley would have it-it is, rather, to deny the distinction between subject and object entirely. There is only the life-expanding process (will to power). This thesis does not deny the existence of spiritual values; it is not "materialistic" (section 37). We may have misunderstood ourselves and the nature of the world completely; but as we become aware of this misunderstanding, it becomes a thing of the past.

39-44. Truth is not necessarily limited to whatever brings about happiness. Truth is independent of pleasure and pain. The free spirit must have the strength to withstand the possible dangers of truth. That which serves the will to power and creativity does not necessarily bring pleasure or happiness.

The free spirit has a need to cast his deeper thoughts into a "mask" - sometimes even in a very coarse form, which is easily misunderstood. This is a psychological need, for his depth renders him vulnerable. The free spirit cannot open himself fully to others, because this renders him dependent upon them, in a way. But he cannot develop without criticism, so he must be self-testing. He has to avoid possible avenues of escape or rationalization, which threaten him by affording a way out of self-responsibility. He shuns extreme sympathy, involvement in a science, or setting up his own freedom or his own virtue as a fixed pursuit. His independence must be complete and free from "crutches."

Nietzsche believes that philosophers who approach this ideal may now be developing. They will maintain a certain obscurity, and might be called "tempters." They will, no doubt, still seek truth. But they will be independent and will reject dogmatism. Such free thinkers, however, must not be confused with philosophical "liberals," socialists, democrats, or others who advocate equality of rights (these, it is true, may reject dogmatism-but only in order to defeat the forces presently in power; see Zarathustra, part two, Of the Tarantulas). By their very nature, doctrines of "equality" do not rise "beyond good and evil."

3 The Religious Mood

45. Any unfettered research into man's inner life, research which is free from philosophical and moral prejudices, must necessarily be the result of individual effort. This is an area where mutual cooperation is difficult, since it involves the soul of the investigator himself, and therefore, as a form of self-criticism, requires a strong nature. As Nietzsche said in section 23, such research "has the heart against it." An honest investigation of the religious experience of man, therefore, has to be an individual effort. It requires an investigator who has himself experienced much of the religious life.

46-49. Christian faith is primarily a matter of sacrifice and subjection. Cruelty and pain are its basic attributes, and these arise from the imprisonment of the spirit. The Christian symbol of the crucified God represented, more than anything else, a destruction of previous, aristocratic ideals. Christianity, as a revolt of slaves against tyrants, was motivated primarily by the resentment which the slaves felt for their masters, because the aristocracy was indifferent to pain.

Religion, or the "religious neurosis," as a form of institutionalized suffering, has generally been marked by the presence of sexual abstinence, fasting, and solitude. It is neither possible nor desirable to attempt to establish a causal connection between these ideals and religion. A more interesting question is: how is it possible to impose such stringent restrictions upon fundamental human instincts? This question reaches its height in the case of the saint, who achieves a sort of spiritual transformation as a result of extreme self-denial. This phenomenon has been widely regarded as miraculous or supernatural; but it may be that the reason for such an "explanation" is simply the inability to conceive of the possibility that a good thing can arise from a bad one-a form of the prejudice of moral opposites.

Southern, or Latin races, find it more difficult to tolerate religious unbelief, perhaps because the "spirit of the race" is religious, while northern races, with the possible exception of the Celts, are more instinctively barbarous. For the ancient Greeks, religion was marked originally by a feeling of gratitude, a sign of their racial vigor. Later on, this feeling was replaced by an attitude of fear (the result of the slave revolt). (See also the comment following section 3 above.)

50. The "passion for God" takes many forms: straightforward and peasantlike, refined exaltation, even tender and sensual. Nietzsche suggests that there may be a sexual element present in this sentiment.

51. The reason that even powerful rulers have respected the saint is that they have sensed the presence of power in such a man. His ability to subjugate himself is a sign of great strength, and they instinctively respect it just as they respect their own strength. Further, the willingness of the saint to subject himself to pain and deprivation arouses a suspicion that the saint knows of something to be gained, which he keeps secret. This may even produce a fear of the saint.

52. The Jewish "Old Testament" is a remarkable book, with a depth and breadth of experience which is unmatched even by Eastern religious texts. The New Testament, on the other hand, is poor and petty in spirit, not worthy of consideration alongside the other.

Comment

In *The Genealogy of Morals*, third essay, 22, Nietzsche attacks the New Testament as representative of a corruption of literary taste brought about by the ideals of asceticism.

53-55. The rise of atheism is not necessarily a sign of religious decline, but of the failure of the theistic interpretation of things. God as the father-figure and reward-giver has failed to manifest himself. Modern philosophy, also, has contributed to anti-Christian sentiment by attacking the idea of the "soul" on epistemological grounds (the soul cannot be known). But it is not thereby antireligious. (Kant held that a transcendent soul cannot be known to exist objectively, but he still supported religious values.)

Religious faith, as cruelty and sacrifice, has produced, perhaps, a significant tendency toward atheism. From the sacrifice of human beings to the sacrifice of their strongest instincts (through asceticism and antinaturalism), there may develop a third stage: the sacrifice of God Himself, as the dearest possession of man.

Comment

This passage affords grounds for looking upon "the ugliest man" in part four of Zarathustra, who admits to the "murder" of God, as representing atheism. However, it should be noted that it is not atheism that destroys God, but the death of God that produces atheism. In neither case is the religious neurosis destroyed.

56-57. Any serious inquiry into the nature of pessimism will reveal, as a result, the nature of the optimistic as well. The optimistic affirms the world as it is, with its possibilities for change. His affirmation reaches its peak when he is willing to accept the possibility of an eternal recurrence of all things, As man's intellectual horizons expand, so does his world, and the views of the past appear small in contrast. It may be that the ideas of God and Sin will fade into insignificance at some future time. It is not necessary that the inclination to seek pain - the religious neurosis - will also disappear.

Comment

Nietzsche's point, in the last few sections, should be clear: atheism and the religious attitude are not opposed to one another.

58-60. A certain inactivity, as far as external affairs are concerned, is necessary for the promotion of a religious life. Modern-day emphasis upon "busy-ness," work, play, scholarship, and in a word, intense activity in all walks of life has a tendency to inhibit the growth of religious life.

Man instinctively has a fear of truth, and is inclined to falsify things as a means of avoiding truth. Philosophers who entertain the fantasy that the real world consists of "pure forms" are in this class. Artists, too, are inclined to oversimplify and distort reality as an escape from truth. Perhaps the highest manifestation of this inclination is the religious man. The religious interpretation of existence represents a deep fear that the truth will have no other result than pessimism and the destruction of man. The love of mankind for the sake of God, too, may reflect a fear that unassisted love will prove impossible.

61-62. The philosopher, in accepting responsibility for the improvement of man, should take into consideration the usefulness of religion. Religion has a fourfold utility:

1. It assists rulers, by establishing a common bond between them and their subjects.

2. It affords an institutionalized place of retreat for higher natures who desire a contemplative life.

3. It establishes a channel through which individuals in the lower classes may attain to intellectual development and command.

4. It extends a certain peace of mind to those masses whose lot it is in life to serve and to work.

However, this last, preservative characteristic of religion can also be a bad thing, because it can upset the natural progress of man by keeping sick elements in society alive, and by presenting a force which opposes the creative gestures of gifted and powerful individuals. In this respect, religion may be a factor in the deterioration of man.

4 Apothegms And Interludes

Comment

As explained in the Introduction, this section, which consists of brief, epigrammatic comments, will be omitted (sections 63-185).

It is not difficult to relate these passages to the remainder of the book. For example, number 75, "The degree and nature of a man's sensuality extends to the highest altitudes of his spirit," may be readily associated with the thesis in number 50, that the passion for God has an element of sensuality in it. It is also related to Nietzsche's general thesis that the spiritual and the physical are not opposites.

5 The Natural History Of Morals

186-187. Current attempts (1885) to construct a reasoned theory of morals are doomed to failure, because they do not have the meticulous and careful outlook which fits the extremely complex nature of the subject. Any theory of morals requires, first of all, a detailed study of the great variety of ways in which value manifests itself-a study of "distinctions of worth." This is necessary only as a preparation. Present theory suffers from a lack of knowledge of the subject (and a consequent oversimplification). It presumes to provide a solid foundation for morals, without fully understanding the real problems which arise when many different moralities are brought to light. Current theories end up by merely supporting a simple version of the moral attitudes of the day.

It is always enlightening to seek out the source of a moral judgment in the temperament of the individual who proposes it. Systems of morals may reflect a desire for self-justification, for example, or a need for revenge, or for humility. Immanuel Kant, certainly, reflected a great inclination toward obedience. Moral "systems" may simply be a reflection of the emotional life of the system-builder.

Comment

In modern times, some philosophers have taken this idea of a relation between emotions and moral judgments to be defining. They hold that moral judgments are no more than an expression of emotion. An example of this point of view is to be found in Chapter 6 of *Language, Truth and Logic*, by A. J. Ayer (Dover Publications, New York.) Nietzsche, however, does not seem to be in agreement with this idea, as the following passages make clear.

188-189. The essential element in a true moral system is its imposition of discipline and restraint. Man's "natural" state is not one of uninhibited freedom, but one in which an arbitrarily imposed control is accepted for the sake of a higher freedom.

Comment

Nietzsche means this quite literally. He associates the presence of such restraints with the natural conditions for the existence of a living organism. Further discussion of this point occurs in section 230 below.

The artist, for example, subjects himself to a complex set of rules, in order to achieve that power over a certain sphere which is his art. Only after a period of intense discipline is he able to "create" - to exhibit that creative flair which is called "freedom." Where freedom of choice, responsibility, and spiritual creativity are concerned-in short, where morals are concerned, a disciplining with regard to human and social actions is necessary. Such a need for discipline is also "natural" in the sense that the medium in which it is to take place imposes its own laws, which govern the case (for example, freedom and wide range of ability in playing the guitar must derive from a strict observance of the qualitative character of vibrating strings). It is the same with social and spiritual freedom. The imposition of fasts and of abstinence from various forms of activity can result in a subsequent improvement of that activity, when it is resumed. Many "holidays" are really disguised fasts, after which the worker finds his skill refreshed. It is even possible that entire periods of history, during which strict moral restraints have been imposed, have functioned as fasting periods, after which the restrained instincts re-emerge in a higher form. The sublimation of sexual instincts into Christian love is an example.

Comment

This has a bearing on the question asked in section 47: "How is the saint possible?" The appearance of high spiritual qualities out of self-discipline is of the same order as the transformation of muscular activity into the beauty of the dance-both are accomplished by discipline and a lengthy period of restraint. The amazing bodily disciplines in Yoga, for example, appear to have a similar purpose.

These two passages (188-189) contain some of Nietzsche's most interesting insights. They are among the first hints that the human phenomenon of the ability to learn-to transform natural habit patterns by learning to act and react according to rules-is of great importance to moral theory. The suggestion that the principles which govern learning discipline are derived, in part at least, from the natural conditions of the medium, (in morals, the social medium), is a viewpoint which goes counter to the historical idea that moral principles are derived from external standards. It is also a reflection of the impact of scientific method, which derives its principles from the observed behavior of its subject matter. For further research, see R. M. Hare, *The Language of Morals* (chapter, "Moral Reasoning," reprinted in *Knowledge and Value*, ed. Sprague and Taylor; Harcourt, Brace and World, New York, 1959).

190-191. The Socratic view that the source of evil is error, since no man really desires to injure himself (and all evil is ultimate self-injury), is a form of Utilitarianism, the moral theory which places pursuit of happiness uppermost. Such theories of avoidance of pain and pursuit of pleasure are derived from the sentiments of the general public, the "followers" rather than the "leaders." Theories of morality which place the origin of value in a rational standard, rather than in irrational instinct (reason rather than faith), also reflect public sentiment, because reason is developed with a view to utility and goal-seeking. Plato, who observed that valuations have an irrational element, sought at least to prove that the rational and the irrational would lead to the same conclusion. Hence, he identified the "true" and the "good." Descartes, on the other hand, denied the instinctual entirely, and placed his confidence in reason alone.

192-193. The development of any science shows that even simple observation is largely structured by our predispositions and beliefs. In a sense, we see only what we want to see - the faculty of perception is not a cold mirror of events, but a "mirror" whose curves are introduced by emotion and valuation. What we observe is often simplified, and so falsified, by our habits (new sciences are often forced to overcome this observational impediment before they can progress). Even our dream experiences are capable of altering our waking perceptions.

194-196. A simple itemization of the things that people find desirable is not a sufficient guide to their values; there is a question remaining, namely: what do they mean by "having," or "possessing," those things? The meaning of these terms is not always clear, nor is it always the same

Comment

For example, it may be said that a people desires "freedom"; but until their conception of what it would be like to have freedom is revealed, we know very little. Nietzsche here exhibits his philological background, by showing sensitivity to the importance of crucial terms-a habit which has become highly developed in modern times. He concludes section 194 with a detailed discussion of the meaning of "possession." His main emphasis, however, is upon morals: the real nature of a value system is only revealed by its practice (what the possession of the valued things is like), rather than by its theory.

The slave revolt in morals, which Nietzsche attributes to the Jews, was an inversion of previous values. Things which had been considered "good," such as riches, became "evil" instead. Even the word "world" became a term of negative import. The significance of this inversion of values is not to be looked for "on the surface" (any more than a term like "freedom" can be understood, in the mouth of another, until his behavior is observed). Nietzsche therefore begins a detailed investigation of what he terms the "morals of timidity."

197-199. Moralists who condemn the violent and commanding elements of nature, including the powerful man (such a man as Caesar Borgia), reveal a misunderstanding of nature itself. Their standard of value lies in the temperate and the mediocre; particularly, in the happiness of the masses. Such theories are a manifestation of fear, and a reflection of the presence of outside dangers. They are poor, theoretically, because they attempt to apply a single standard to all members of society, and even to all societies; something that cannot really work. They ignore, suppress, or otherwise channel the emotions, merely as a matter of freedom and expediency.

In human societies, there has always been a distinction between the larger, obedient masses - the "herd" - and those who are leaders. The masses, of course, are the larger group, and their chief characteristics is obedience. The habit of obedience, as a result, has stamped itself upon mankind to the extent that the need for it is almost an instinct. Nietzsche is of the opinion that man has not progressed as far as he might have, and one of the reasons, he believes, is that the instinct for obedience is more readily perpetuated than the instinct to command (see section 62 for the role of religion in this connection).

This instinct to obey, Nietzsche speculates, may grow to the point where even the leaders are under its sway. At this point, they will attempt to make their leadership seem as if it is a form of obedience; a subordination, for example, to a constitution, or to the will of the people. Those qualities that are highly prized by the masses, such as public spirit and modesty, will also become virtues in the leader. An ultimate development of this tendency is the replacement of leaders by groups of nonleaders, whose joint decision will be governing. Napoleon was a refreshing exception to this trend.

200. In conjunction with his view that there can be an "inherited" instinct for obedience, Nietzsche expresses the notion that moral sentiments in general may be transmitted by heredity, even as a racial characteristic. In the man of mixed race, he suggests, there may occur a psychological conflict, owing to the presence of conflicting moral sentiments which derive from his mixed origin. Such conflict generally produces a weak

individual, who may seize upon "happiness" as a way out. It can, however, produce the opposite - the powerful man, whenever there is also present an inherited ability of self-mastery.

201. The utilitarian quality of the "morals of timidity" is directed toward a single end, the preservation and contentment of the group. As long as this is the case, the ideal of "love of one's neighbor" cannot be truly achieved. At first, sympathetic tendencies toward other members of the group are simply accepted, not valued in a moral sense. As the group becomes secure the primary emotion governing human relations becomes fear. The characteristics of the fighting man, developed as part of the protection of the group, become a source of internal insecurity. A new moral perspective arises, one which condemns elements of power and creativity, since these shake the confidence of the community in its stability. In contrast, all moderate elements become praiseworthy. This stage, again, is dominated by fear, not by love. As this trend continues, eventually violence even in the prosecution of the law becomes a source of disturbance. Severe punishments are avoided, and criminals receive the benefit of increasing support on the part of the legal system.

Comment

The account of these stages in the development of the "morals of timidity" is expanded in *The Genealogy of Morals* (second essay, sections 7-10).

202. Nietzsche makes it clear that his use of the term "herd" in referring to the utilitarian moral system is not intended as a **metaphor**, but is meant to express his general belief that human social systems are not fundamentally separate from those of

animals. The unanimity of moral sentiment throughout Europe, the certainty that the knowledge of good and evil is complete, can only be described, he says, as a development of the herd instinct. Other moralities are possible, but the herd morality defends itself by laying claim to the final truth. Religion has assisted this, and democratic social systems have resulted.

Even anarchism (which supports the abolition of any formal government), as it presents itself today, is not really removed from the influence of this herd morality. The anarchist, in supporting rule of the individual by the individual, seems to be opposed to socialists and "equalizers"; but in fact both factions are agreed in that they are antagonistic toward class distinctions; they oppose special privileges; they share an aversion for legal punishment; they value sympathy; and they fear suffering.

203. If it is accepted that democratic political systems are basically a weakening influence, where is a strong counterforce to be found? Nietzsche places his hope in the emergence of the new philosopher. Such men, he hopes, will introduce a new order of values; they will emphasize man's responsibility for his own future. Above all, they will attempt to free man from submission to historical accident, which has been the governing factor in his progress so far. In the next chapter, Nietzsche deals with the new philosopher in greater detail.

BEYOND GOOD AND EVIL

TEXTUAL ANALYSIS

PART 6 AND 7

| 6 We Scholars

204-206. The man of science is not to be placed above the philosopher in order of rank. Scientists, under the influence of the democratic spirit which demands freedom from all masters, has declared its separation from religion, and now wishes to take the place of philosophy as the highest discipline. It is not difficult, indeed, to construct "insolent" criticism of philosophy. The philosopher does not appear to be a hard worker; the history of philosophy appears to be a history of failures; philosophy may even be mistaken for a form of mysticism. Those who reject the views of a particular philosopher may be led to reject philosophy as a whole, especially if they agreed with that philosopher's own criticism of others. This, however, is merely the result of the weaknesses of present-day philosophy, which has been reduced to mere scholarship, specialization, and overconcern with the theory of knowledge.

It is not easy for the philosopher to achieve a position of prominence. Science, which grows larger and larger, overshadows him with a great body of knowledge. His best way out is specialization, but this is fundamentally opposed to the philosophical instinct. The philosopher is committed to judgments regarding life, and this imposes upon him a duty to seek out depth of experience. The public is often misled by this trait; they identify anyone who lives apart, such as the scientist, scholar, or priest, with the philosopher. But the real philosopher is not of this stamp at all-he seeks experience, and therefore does not live "prudently," but in great spiritual danger, for he questions even himself.

The scientific man differs from the creative genius. He rules out sensual pleasure and the virtues of command, and instead glorifies the mediocre values of industry, adaptability, and moderation. He is in constant need of self-justification, which stems from the distrust and envy characteristic of all dependent classes (see section 260).

207-209. The objective point of view is valuable, but there is a danger in taking it as an end, and not as a means. The scientist, by his very nature, deals in generalities. This isolation from the concrete case makes it difficult for him to affirm or deny personal values. His emotions suffer, as a result, and he can neither love nor hate without restraint. He is, in other words, removed from questions of value: his function is therefore instrumental, and does not reach into deep human issues.

The philosopher who does not advocate some form of scepticism is the unusual case, and people may fear him, because he is difficult to understand. In the presence of widespread nihilistic feeling, scepticism is one of the best "sedatives." The sceptical point of view permits a suspension of judgment, and thereby protects the sceptic from the responsibility of affirming or denying values.

Scepticism is a form of physiological weakness. It is exemplary of the weakness of will which results from the blending of classes and races, with its consequent confusion of moral instincts. The power of will is weakest in France, stronger in Germany and England; it is strongest in Russia. Europe will need a powerful antidote in order to compete with Russia for future supremacy. The twentieth century will witness a great struggle in world politics, a struggle for world dominion on the part of a new ruling class. There is, however, a stronger form of scepticism-a "masculine" scepticism-which is German in character. This is a fatalistic acceptance of a lack of values, coupled with aggressive tendencies, which produces a certain freedom and will to conquer. This warlike German scepticism is a factor which must be appreciated.

210-211. But the new philosophers will not be sceptics, in either sense. They might better be called critics. The critic differs from the sceptic in his affirmative spirit toward value standards, his experimental attitude (which is a form of courage), and his ability to accept responsibility. The new philosopher will not love truth for the sake of pleasure or spiritual enrichment; he will not identify the true with the beautiful or the "good." Such a view is foolish romanticism. The philosopher's concern with truth is, rather, a direct expression of the will to power, and nothing else. "Knowing," for him, is the same as "creating." Nor will the new philosopher concern himself with a reconciliation of conflicting value systems.

But although the philosopher will require great critical ability, he will not consider himself only a critic. Criticism is itself an instrument. The primary task of the philosopher is the creation of values. Even those who formulate systems of values which are simply formalizations of previous value systems, are merely philosophical "workers" and not true philosophers. True philosophy creates new values, and this is the highest expression of the will to power.

Comment

Although Nietzsche's tone here is militant and impassioned, and his use of the term "power" increases the impression of an arbitrary attitude, his insight is a valuable one. The basic element of theory here is the conviction that values are not discovered, but created. The basis for valuation is not to be found in **metaphysical** structures which are independent of man, but in the actions and nature of man himself. The philosopher, then, must not engage in a fruitless search for some mysterious order of the cosmos upon which values are to be based. He must, instead, study man and the experience of man.

Nietzsche's emphasis upon values as a reflection of command, emotion, temperament, physiology, and environmental conditions is not at all strange or arbitrary. It is the keynote of a large part of modern philosophical research, undertaken with the purpose of obtaining a clear understanding of the connection between moral judgments and imperative sentences, expressions of emotion, and the psychology of habit and learning. His view also has an effect upon notions of responsibility. If values are creations and not discoveries, man must accept responsibility for values "on his own"; he can no longer lean upon a supposed "universal order" for support. Because he has this responsibility, and because social and physical conditions change, there can be no fixed order of values. This sense of "abandonment" and lonely responsibility has been a major concern of modern existentialism.

Man, however, has developed an almost instinctive belief in the necessity of fixed values. The conscious recognition that there are none does not wipe out this instinctive pattern, and the result of the ensuing conflict between old habit and conscious belief is a tendency toward pessimism. Scepticism, as Nietzsche describes it above, is one way of "hiding one's head in the sand," refusing to face this conflict. The philosopher must accept man's responsibility, and face it without submitting to pessimism.

212-213. As a creator of values, the philosopher often finds himself in conflict with accepted standards. For example, in this age of specialization and cooperation, he will be inclined to assert the importance of adaptability, confidence in personal decisions, and comprehensiveness.

What a philosopher is cannot be learned easily; it requires experience. The philosopher must achieve the difficult goal of blending boldness with caution. The scholarly ideal emphasizes only the latter of these. Artists, perhaps, come closest to the kind of experience with permits an understanding of the philosophical temperament. In the artist, "necessity" and "freedom of the will" are simply two sides of the same coin. Physiology, temperament, and instinct are as important as intellect in the development of philosophers. Consequently, such men will have to be the product of many generations of development.

Comment

Nietzsche's account of the place of necessity in artistic creation was elaborated in sections 188-189. It is to be noted that his view here, that necessity and free will are not opposed, is another application of his antagonism toward the prejudice of opposites (section 2).

7 Our Virtues

214-217. The spirit of the modern age is one of conflict and indecision. Our virtues, therefore, if we have any, are not to be found as readily as those of our forefathers. Modern man is the inheritor of more than one morality; the moral quality of his actions is often many-sided and unclear. "Love of one's enemies," for example, seems to have developed into a moral standard, but even this operates on an unconscious level, and not as conscious "attitude." This, however, is a superior stage since conscience now comes into play (compare section 32). Those who demand a conscious recognition of their "goodness" are dangerous, because they cannot withstand embarrassment, which they may answer with revenge.

218-219. The best "intelligence" lies on the level of instinct. The internalization of standards (conscience) is more thorough and functional than a continual necessity for conscious referral to standards. Psychologists would do better to study the lower classes, in whom morality has become almost instinctive, than to study superficial "upper-middle-class" behavior.

The conscious exercise of moral condemnation is merely a form of revenge, and reveals the shallow quality of the person who habitually does so. It is really a compensation for poor temperament, but it can be developed into the very opposite (a high spiritual quality) if carried to its utmost. Spirituality develops out of its opposite, shallowness, only through the intervention of a long period of self-imposed moral restraint. Spirituality is, in fact, the opposite side of a continuum, at the other end of which lies justice as a form of revenge. It is, then, the sublimation of revenge; the transformation of a destructive impulse into an ennobling one.

Comment

The function of moral restraint in producing spiritual qualities is discussed in sections 188-189. The passage above, regarding justice and revenge, is a short expression of the main thesis in *The Genealogy of Morals*, second essay.

220-222. The objective spirit, which praises "disinterestedness," is misleading. Disinterested action is not a virtue in itself. It takes on moral quality only as an instrument of an intense interest. The key to the value of disinterestedness lies in a study of what interests higher men. The idea that love should be divorced from egoism is an absurd one, and represents the mistake carried to its extreme. The daring philosopher of the "perhaps" (section 2) may even suppose that "unselfishness" is valuable only as an expression of selfishness, for example, when it is exercised as a right on the part of a powerful individual; he can afford unselfishness, because of his richness. On the other hand, a weaker ego cannot withstand this procedure, and what is good in the former case is evil in the latter. Values differ according to the order of rank. (Note, however, that what establishes this order is just the degree of ability to bestow without losing oneself in the process-see *Thus Spoke Zarathustra*; part one, The Bestowing Virtue.)

Modern man is marked by self-dissatisfaction. His desire to be a "fellow sufferer" is a sign of self-contempt and vanity.

223-225. The ambiguity of modern man regarding value systems, which results from his "hybrid" breeding (see section 214), has caused him to develop a historical sense. He looks eagerly into history in a restless search for a "form" which may be given his unformed morality. At the same time, he has attained a perspective regarding historical moralities, such that he is able to take them with a grain of salt, even laugh at them.

This historical sense shows itself in the increasing ability to understand literature embodying a variety of moral sentiments. Modern appreciation of Homer (ca. 850 B.C.) exemplifies this. We can also "stomach" a confusing synthesis of tastes, as is plainly evident in our appreciation of Shakespeare. This historical sense is one of our great virtues; it carries with it hostility to "finished" cultures, and an experimental attitude. There is a certain affirmation of the unmeasurable or unfixed, which may constitute a force opposed to the traditional over-valuation of certainty and stability.

This experimental, "open-ended" attitude is a dangerous one, but it is also a welcome one; it accepts the danger which is a part of all true creativity. Systems which avoid danger and seek pleasure or well-being are destructive to the creative spirit. Man is both a creature (something passive because created: creature) and a creator. As a creature, he desires well-being; but as a creator, he must not turn away from suffering.

226-228. Those who think and work "beyond good and evil," and who may be called "immoralists," have their own sense of duty. Honesty, perhaps, is their inescapable virtue. Free spirits should perfect their honesty, if they cannot avoid it, but they must not let it become a wearisome burden.

Until now, moral philosophy has been noncreative. The English Utilitarians (for example, John Stuart Mill) contribute nothing original. They do not even take proper care in inspecting the history of moral sentiments. They merely rationalize the attempt to dictate English morality to the world as a whole. This morality, with its emphasis upon well-being, provides no positive goals. It is essentially a prohibitive morality, not a creative one.

229-231. However frightening it may be, one must acknowledge the base origins of humanity; the wild beast is still present in man. The desire for cruelty, which stems from enjoyment taken in the suffering of others and even of oneself, has not been eradicated from man's soul. It has simply been transformed, and is represented, for example, in "culture" by the aesthetic pleasure of the tragic drama. Religious self-denial and the rigorous self-discipline of the scientist are other manifestations of this sublimation of cruelty. Cruelty, in turn, is one aspect of the will to power, as it appears in every living thing. This will may be analyzed in the following manner:

1. Growth. The living thing assimilates alien factors in the environment, rejecting that which it finds inimical or inconsequential, and accepting the useful. It orders and arranges things according to the most useful scheme. This ordering is the prototype of that falsification and simplification which in man is language and science (see section 24).

2. Defense. The negative side of this arbitrary arrangement of things is a system of prohibitions, the refusal to admit variations beyond certain limits. The spirit resembles the "stomach," which will only digest certain things, allowing others to pass by untouched and unrecognized.

3. Deception. In social contexts, where other creatures are involved, this self-deception (in 2 above) becomes a deception of others, for the sake of the security which this provides.

4. Cruelty. Since severe discipline is a necessary condition for ability to arrange things freely and creatively (sections 24 and 188), a certain self-restriction (and even group restriction), which is a form of cruelty, is also a part of the pattern of life. Man gives this aspect high-sounding titles, such as "sacrifice for knowledge," but these highest things are rooted in falsification and cruelty.

Comment

A very similar account of such a "pattern" occurs in John Dewey's book, *Logic: The Theory of Inquiry*, in the chapter entitled "The Biological Matrix of Inquiry."

All adaptation, learning, and growth, however, has a center, a core, which does not alter. Our firmest convictions are more valuable as revelations of our own deepest emotional temper than they are as truths (see section 187). Convictions are merely symptoms of our valuations; and it is our valuations which tell us what we truly are.

Comment

This view, that there is a relatively fixed temperament underlying external behavior, should not be confused with the belief in a soul. Nietzsche has rejected the latter idea (section 12).

232-239. Nietzsche concludes with a discussion of woman. He does not approve of the "democratic" tendency to intellectualize woman. She is not a thinker; she has always avoided truth-her greatest skill is that of ornamentation.

Intellectual women are merely "comical." Ornament is the means which woman employs toward her primary end: this is, man (but in *Zarathustra*, Nietzsche stated that man was the means to the end, which was pregnancy). The real basis for the male-female relationship is antagonism. Woman is the possession, man the possessor; woman must be kept, like a fragile bird-man is the keeper. If woman loses her fear of man, she will lose all femininity. Man, also, has a certain fear of woman, for she represents the irrational, the unpredictable. The breakdown of these basically instinctive relations is a sign of the degeneracy introduced by the democratization of Europe.

BEYOND GOOD AND EVIL

TEXTUAL ANALYSIS

PART 8 AND 9

....

8 Peoples And Countries

240-243. Germany today exhibits a certain two-sided character, as a nation and a race. Just as German music is both ancient and modern in feeling, so the German spirit is both young and old. There is a lack of definiteness, but a great potentiality. The German spirit also exhibits a certain element of deliberate clumsiness, a lack of "southern" gracefulness.

There is a tendency for Europeans to be seized by moments of petty and narrow patriotism. But beneath external affairs, there is a growing tendency toward the development of a supernational sort of man. The mixing of races and moralities produces a type of man independent of the cultural and environmental conditions which are characteristic of nations and races. As a result of this process, conditions are favorable for the appearance of men of exceptional character, as well as those of mediocre ability. The tyrant, as well as the slave, can be the result of "democratic" mixing of races (see section 200). The key to this possibility of opposites arising from the same source is the great adaptability which the supernatural man must have.

244. Germans have been thought of as a "deep" race. What does this "depth" amount to? As has been said, the German spirit has a "mixed" source, and because of this it is difficult to define the German. The keynote of the German character is development. As a race and as a nation, Germany is in a period of transition. The rumor of German "depth" is partly an expression of this fact. Germans are also slow and clumsy, and they take a long time to "digest" anything. This characteristic is also a source of the idea of German "depth." It is well, however, for a people to have a public "face"; development takes place under such deception (see sections 223 and 240).

245. Regarding German music: Beethoven represents the transition of Germany, the middle ground between light classicism (Mozart) and the music of modern youthfulness. In Beethoven, there is a feeling of both loss and hope-loss of an older taste, hope for the new. Romanticism after Beethoven was a superficial interlude, in which Felix Mendelssohn was a rare brightness. The music of Robert Schumann is simply something that is best left behind, for it is not sufficiently supernational. (For Nietzsche, Richard Wagner approached this supernational ideal. See sections 255 and 256.)

246-247. Regarding the German language: Germans have not generally come to an understanding of the way in which writing can express rhythm and tempo (see sections 27-28). But such an understanding is really necessary for an understanding of the meaning of sentences. A tasteful literature must harmonize meaning with tempo. A sign that Germans do not understand this is the general tendency to read silently, and to separate the spoken style from the written style. This was not the case in ancient times. In present-day Germany, the nearest approximation to the ancient ideal, in which breath and thought are in harmony, is to be found in the church. The German Bible (Luther's Bible) is, perhaps, the "best German book."

248-249. Just as there are active and passive creative men (see the Comment following the Dance Song in *Thus Spoke Zarathustra*), there are also active and passive nations. Some bring forth new things (the Greeks, the French) and others form the material for later development (the Jews, Romans, and perhaps the Germans). Often nations do not recognize their own role, because they have a tendency to take superficial characteristics too seriously.

250-251. Regarding the Jews: Europe owes the Jews a great debt of gratitude, if only because they originated the powerful, disciplinary moral spirit. Anti-Semitism in Europe is a folly, a lapse similar to the "patriotism" mentioned in section 241. These "follies" are difficult to avoid, because they depend upon temperament, and it is not likely that Germans will ever be able to overcome them. The Jews are a tremendously strong race, and there is a natural fear of them among weaker Europeans. Both the Jews and the Russians have a capacity for slow adaptation which is an integral part of their strength. Their powerful nature could give them the control of Europe, but they do not desire this, whatever anti-Semites, may say. Europe could benefit more from the Jews, and it might be a good idea to put an end to anti-Semitism.

252-253. Regarding England: The English are not a creative philosophical race. They are too mechanical. English music reflects this; it never "gets off the ground." Only the most mediocre European intellects can be taken in by English thought, and it has some influence upon middle-class taste in Europe. This is not a bad thing, because it stimulates a certain amount of detail work which can be helpful to the genuine creator. Real creators will not be such "workers" (see section 211), and they may even be "ignorant" in strictly scientific matters.

254-255. Regarding France: Although France presents a rather crude face to modern Europe, it is still the heart of the most refined culture. The French, however, cannot avoid pessimism, and German thought, especially that of Schopenhauer, has a great influence in France. The French have a great amount of artistic sentiment, a refined psychological insight, and a blending of northern and southern temperaments which permits depth without gloominess. The music of Bizet expresses this southern character. German music, with its antagonism to southern lightness, is dangerous; if it were released from its extreme northern iciness, a truly super-European music might arise.

256. The influence of nationalism in Europe obscures the real tendency of Europe to become a single unit. But the greater men of the century, such as Napoleon, Goethe, and Beethoven, were preparations for the coming unity. Richard Wagner, himself, reflects this; his work is not nationalistic, and has a strong French influence. These great men are the prototypes of the European to come.

9 What Is Noble?

257-259. The "elevation" of man is dependent entirely upon the existence of aristocratic societies, in which there is an order of rank among the populace, and a servile class at the bottom. Out of the sense of separation of class from class (a "pathos of distance"), there may arise a sense of "distance" within the soul, a desire for "higher states." Under the influence of this desire, man finds a way to mount higher and higher, through self-overcoming. The unpleasant truth of the matter is that such aristocratic societies have only resulted from the conquering of a weaker race by a stronger.

The ruling class must not consider itself as a servant of the state, but rather as the very goal of the state. Society exists only as a means for the production of higher men. Only a corrupt aristocracy considers itself subordinate to the ruling body. The healthy ruling class maintains an aloof autonomy. Any society which takes equality of privilege and will as its basic rule, denies a characteristic of life itself. The essence of life is a kind of exploitation of the weaker by the stronger. This "exploitation" is not an evil, but simply a fact of existence, a "primary organic function," and it is a part of the will to power (see section 230).

260-261. There are two main types of morality: the slave-morality and the master morality.

The Master Morality. The noble man possesses, above all, a proud state of mind, and this pride expresses itself in his active dislike of certain characteristics of the slave class. In this morality, "good" is associated with "noble," and "bad" simply means that which is despised (by the nobles). Cowardice, timidity, overattention to utility, distrustfulness, self-abasement, and dishonesty are all despised by the noble, and are therefore "bad". The noble creates values, and he honors in others those qualities which he himself praises. He may help those of lesser status, but always out of an overflow of his own power, never out of pity. He admires discipline and severity. His primary rule is "faith in oneself." "Duty," for the noble, is not a word which applies equally to all men. He has duties only to those of equal rank.

The Slave Morality. This morality is characterized by a lack of faith in mankind-a pessimistic view of the world. The primary articles of value are those which eliminate as much pain from life as possible; it is, therefore, the morality of utility. Instead of the distinction "good" and "bad", this morality substitutes the distinction "good" and "evil." What is good is what serves to keep suffering at a minimum; what is evil is the power of the ruling class, together with all the qualities which characterize the rulers, such as lack of humility.

To the noble man, vanity is an alien thing. He is careful to estimate his own worth accurately, and to ask of others only this same estimate. The praise of others is valued by him only because he honors them. He does not seek a place in the order of rank that is due to external circumstance or "position." The servile class, on the other hand, accepts outward signs of status as definitive. This is due to their inability to create values. The slave does not form value judgments-he must always have a standard supplied by others. While the vain individual loves to hear good things said of himself, and is hurt by bad comments, the noble man is inclined to reject overestimates of his value, and to appreciate bad opinions an aid to self-improvement.

262. Society passes through several stages in developing the "morals of timidity" (section 197). (1) Under an aristocratic rule, conditions are generally hard; the society has to meet external danger. This severity in the face of external dangers requires a certain uniformity of behavior, and a lack of tolerance for variations. (2) As the society becomes secure, conditions favorable for the appearance of originality and variation develop (it is the experience of animal breeders, says Nietzsche,

that security and abundant food stimulate variations). (3) The strength which was generated by the old "hard" life is now channeled into social dissent, and the old morality will no longer serve as a restraint, since the dangers under which it arose have been removed. (4) This internal dissent presents a new danger, and a new morality is needed to meet it. (5) The new morality will praise the mediocre and will elevate moderation to a position of importance, in order to counteract the effect of internal variation.

263-265. Some individuals have a natural ability to discern the order of rank. Each individual has an innate value, and this can be often discerned by observing how reverent the individual can be. The vulgar tend to blindness, when a beautiful or noble thing is placed before them (like the Bible). The higher individual, on the other hand, shows his appreciation in the presence of such things. The development of noble sentiments depends partly upon an imposed, authoritarian demand that such valuable things be regarded with reverence.

Long-standing ancestral habits cannot be discounted in understanding the behavior of present generations. Ancestry shows itself in the disposition and talents of the young. Democratic education, which attempts to ignore and even eliminate innate (racial) differences, is essentially a deception. The simultaneous praise of truth and "individuality" is hypocritical and contradictory.

A certain egoism is a natural inheritance of the noble soul, and the noble exercises his superiority without evil intent, merely as a form of natural "justice". At the same time, he recognizes his duty to his equals, also as a natural pattern of behavior. He has a deep instinct for maintaining a balance of obligation among those of the same rank. The morality of obligation is not accepted by him as an imposition, but as a right. (Regarding egoism, see also Nietzsche's *Ecce Homo*, Chap. III, 5.)

266-269. Both the self-seeking man and the self-abasing man are distasteful to the noble. What does the opposite, ignobility, really stand for? Above all, it stands for the common. There is a natural tendency in men to evolve toward the common. Language, as a mark of national or racial unity, is itself a powerful factor in promoting a commonality among men, for it depends upon the establishment of a common ground of experience and need. Once again, Nietzsche presents his view that language "falsifies" (compare section 24). As far as survival is concerned, the common people have all the advantage; even language works for them.

It is difficult for a psychologist to study the uncommon cases, because of the danger of being overcome by sympathy. Higher individuals are always "desperate," always faced with destruction. Because of his insight into the nature of the higher man, the psychologist is inclined to view with sympathy and disgust those same men who are often held in reverence by the multitude. The face which the great man presents to popular view is never a true one. Even love is not a sufficient remedy for the inner torment of the great man. The inadequacies of human love, in fact, may have led to the "invention" of the Christian God of pure love.

270-274. Depth of suffering separates the higher man from others, and he protects his position by "disguising" himself in various ways. Apparent attention to pleasure and moderation (Epicureanism), follies, and "science," have all been "masks" by which the higher man conceals himself. The higher man has a sense of "purity" which, in its ultimate form, is holiness. His sensitivity to a lack of purity in others separates him from them.

The saint pities those who are less pure; he who is higher than the saint considers even pity an impurity. The higher man does not share his duties with others-what is an obligation for him need not be one for another. Again, this separates him from others. The man who seeks higher things must also consider others as a means, not as a goal. Solitude is the consequence of these isolating factors - and solitude can be toxic. The higher man is not only alone; he also waits, like a pregnant woman, for the chance set of conditions which will best release his powers. Sometimes he is forced to wait too long, until he becomes too weary to act.

275-279. Those who look only for the worst in a man show a lack of noble sensibility. The noble man, however, requires a complex set of conditions for his very existence. For this reason, lesser men have a better chance of survival. Also, the complexity of the process of self-development, undertaken by the creative spirit, makes it all the more probable that something will be omitted - and therefore be lacking when needed. The extreme sensitivity which the higher man has to his own weaknesses, and his precarious position, forces him to take up an appearance of stability. Noble men often appear to be too happy.

Comment

These are the qualities which Nietzsche has attributed to the noble man: a deep capacity for reverence, continual suffering, inner purity, a sense of duty, loneliness and solitude, constant waiting, complexity, and the ever-present "mask."

280-282. Even Nietzsche's own apparent aggressiveness and extreme views are a kind of "mask," necessary for the maintaining of his inquiring spirit. He himself often has doubts and is severely self-critical, but he continues to search out every possibility-to be a philosopher of the "perhaps." It is not easy to maintain personal integrity in the face of all that is lacking in the world. Disgust with the state of things can catapult a man unexpectedly into madness.

283-286. It is better to praise those with whom one disagrees than to praise one's own views in others. Praise, for the higher man, should not necessarily mean agreement. This, however, requires a great deal of self-control. The higher man must have command of his emotions; he has four virtues: courage, insight, sympathy, and solitude. His most important contributions may be misunderstood for generations, and the virtues of the higher man are designed to take this into account. The greatness of a man, indeed, might be measured by the time it takes for him to be understood. The great man looks down from a height, both of space and time.

287-291. The noble soul is not characterized primarily by actions or "works," but by a deep "reverence for itself." The mask which the noble presents to the world takes many forms. The instinctive intellectual may hide his intellectuality by means of outward "enthusiasm." But what he does not reveal what he is; his solitude itself prevents him from attempting seriously to communicate with the masses. The written opinions of a philosopher, in fact, may conceal his true nature, rather than reveal it. In a way, he would rather be misunderstood. Man is, after all, extremely complex, and the simplicity of his works is necessarily unfaithful to their origin. "Good conscience" is an invention that has the character of a simple mask, and morality itself is a vast simplification, which attempts to reduce the complexity of human relationships to a common formula (see also section 19, on the complexity of the will).

292. The philosopher, who seeks unusual and varied experiences, is under the influence of the conflicting motives of fear and curiosity. Fear may cause him to avoid himself, but curiosity brings him back again.

293. Sympathy is a virtue in the higher nature, but it is a vice in the mediocre man, who sympathizes only to ease his suffering. Only the man who is a master, who has some real control and possession of things and of himself, can exercise a true sympathy-one which is not self-seeking.

294. In spite of the fact that some philosophers, like Thomas Hobbes (1588-1679), have cast doubt upon the value of laughter, it is probable that laughter, and even an ability to ridicule the most serious things, is a mark of the truly philosophical spirit.

295. Nietzsche concludes by reaffirming his admiration for the god Dionysos, whom he had praised, as representative of the irrational well-springs of creativity in man, in *The Birth of Tragedy*. In his later book, *Ecce Homo*, he refers to this passage as an example of psychological analysis (Ecce Homo, Chap. III, 6). The god Dionysos is the "genius of the heart," who perpetually requires that a man look into himself for that which is there, but unrecognized and perhaps unformed. As such, this god is the source of self-renewal, even as he is associated with the ceremonies of spring.

Comment

Nietzsche's description of the god, here, however, is somewhat different from that given in his earlier book. There, Dionysos represented mystical contact with the **metaphysical** roots of Being, and a meeting with Dionysos was characterized by a loss of individuality. Here, Dionysos is called a "philosopher," and some have understood Nietzsche as meaning to modify his previous view by adding a Socratic element, an element of rationality, to the former picture of the god. This "god," it is suggested, is a combination of the old Dionysos of pure irrational Being, and the Socrates of critical thought. However, Nietzsche also says here that the role of "investigator" is spurned by Dionysos as simply another "mask," by means of which humans give him a form. The significance, then, of Nietzsche's **allusion** to Dionysos as a "philosopher" is not entirely clear. It seems certain, however, that Dionysos represents a principle which can urge a man toward that self-criticism which brings him to self-knowledge. When Nietzsche called this passage a kind of psychological analysis, he had at least this much in mind.

The characteristics which he attributes here to Dionysos are of some further interest. The god (1) can reach into the depths of a soul, (2) always has an element of motive associated with his appearance, (3) never appears "as he is," (4) condemns superficiality, (5) teaches hesitance and delicacy, and (6) leads to self-enrichment through self-renewal.

Of these, (2) is of particular note. It suggests an element of ego or self, which is contrary to the notion of Dionysos as an embodiment of mystical selflessness. The passage, however, is poetic and even ambiguous; but in section 231, Nietzsche suggested that there is in every man an inner core of self, which lies unchanging at the bottom of all convictions, and which is "unteachable." If this core is that which Dionysos reaches for, it may be speculated that Nietzsche meant to replace the generalized notion of an all-embracing **metaphysical** "Being" by an individualized core of Being; a pluralistic view, then, instead of a monistic one: the universe contains many Dionysiac "Beings," rather than one. This, however, is only an hypothesis.

For the student who is interested in pursuing this further, it may be mentioned that Nietzsche's doctrine that no individual is wholly free from hereditary racial patterns of behavior is relevant to the thesis that each individual has his own inner core of temperament. It means that this "core," while individual, must still partake of as generality, which is the element of racial unity. In section 257, Nietzsche introduces the idea of an "ever new widening of distance within the soul," which he associates with a social structure. There is no doubt that the sum of passages like these leads toward psychological theories such as those of the psychologist C. G. Jung (1875-1961), whose concept of the "collective unconscious" comes particularly close to Nietzsche's thought. (See C. G. Jung, Aion; in *Psyche and Symbol*, ed. V. Laszlo, Anchor Books, New York, 1958).

296. Nietzsche's final comment is an impassioned expression of the fleeting inadequacy of thought and language. His own ideas, like "sudden sparks and marvels," are no sooner expressed, than they are extinguished. Like all art, the work itself captures no eternal truths, but only brilliant moments in the never-ending rush of time. Yet they are not, for all that-less beloved.

BEYOND GOOD AND EVIL

ESSAY QUESTIONS AND ANSWERS

Question: What is the "Will to Power," and how is it related to self-overcoming?

Answer. The Will to Power is the spontaneous inclination of any organism to enlarge and control its sphere of interactions with other things. At any level of animal life, the successful accomplishment of this requires a certain degree of self-control. Such necessary self-control is a form of suffering. For this reason, Nietzsche holds that the basic motivation of all human action is not mere survival, and it is not the pursuit of pleasure, but rather the creative alteration of the environment (and the Self). The ultimate expression of the Will to Power is the creation of values. In man, the creation of values can only come about after a long period of self-restraint, in which the natural instincts and passions of the soul are released from the bonds imposed by morality, transformed by means of self-control, and a stage of affirmation of one's own value judgments is reached. This release, transformation, and control of deep instincts is called self-overcoming, or "sublimation." It is, therefore, an essential part of the expression of the Will to Power in its highest form (the creation of values). Nietzsche says that only the man who can command himself can command others. But the will to Power does not, primarily, refer to worldly power or the domination of others by force. Those who create values will naturally lead the masses, who cannot create, and who need the guidance provided by values. But among the higher men, who are creators, a strict sense of duty and of natural obligation is present. One of the chief implications of Nietzsche's doctrine that the Will to Power is man's basic motivation, is that it leads to a rejection of the Utilitarian ethical system, which teaches that pleasure is the main ethical guidepost. Nietzsche contrasts "pleasure," which is only a value for the masses, with "joy," in which an element of suffering is present, and which is the reward of the Superman.

Question: Explain Nietzsche's analysis of the function of the chorus in Greek tragic drama.

Answer: Nietzsche does not agree with the view of the early nineteenth-century critic A. W. Schlegel that the chorus, which stands between the spectators and the players, symbolizes an "ideal spectator". Nor does he think that it represents the common man. The tragic drama, he says, is a concrete representation (an Apollonian "image" of the deep, irrational forces in nature (the Dionysian "reality"). Just as the players represent the image, the chorus represents the Dionysian reality. If the spectator is allowed to identify with the actors, the artistic quality of the work would be destroyed. The chorus intervenes, and the spectator can identify the chorus instead. But, as a "selfless" multitude, the chorus does not support any given identity, but rather becomes a symbol of the loss of ego which is the essence of the Dionysian reality-lack of individuality. At the same time, the chorus is the source of the **imagery** which appears on the stage; it represents the only reality, and the play itself is merely the momentary expression of that reality. In this way, the spectator participates, to a degree, in the production of the image, since he becomes a part of the chorus.

Question: What is "The Bestowing Virtue"?

Answer. The bestowing virtue is a form of selfishness which leads to the bestowing of benefits upon others. This kind of selfishness is to be sharply contrasted with that which is usually meant by the term. The selfishness of the man who has not gained control of his baser instincts (through "self-overcoming") is a bad form of selfishness, for it is a spirit of mere acquisition, and never benefits anyone else. Only the higher man, who has sublimated his instincts and has obtained command over himself, can accumulate his spiritual riches to the point where they "overflow" and benefit others. Selfishness is a virtue in the Superman, but a vice in the masses.

Nietzsche was against the form of self-denial taught by Christianity, and he felt that man should not be encouraged to feel shame at self-affirmation. But he was also aware of the fact that this doctrine might be mistaken for selfishness of the "lower" sort, and become an excuse for unwarranted egotism. He is very careful, therefore, to point out that only the man who undergoes a severe process of self-criticism and self-overcoming can afford to be truly selfish (the process described in Of the Three Metamorphoses, in part one of *Zarathustra*). In such a man, however, self-enrichment leads directly to an "overflow" of benefits. Since the man who has overcome himself is a creator of values, part of the importance of the bestowing virtue is that it is a giving of new values and new perspectives to others, who may not be able to create values for themselves.

Question: Discuss the doctrine of Eternal Recurrence.

Answer: The doctrine of Eternal Recurrence is the theory that every event in a person's life recurs over and over again, forever (exactly the same way each time). Nietzsche supports this by means of the theory that the universe is infinite in time and space. Since it is infinite, he concludes, an infinite number of possibilities must have occurred an infinite number of times.

Nietzsche feels that acceptance of this doctrine redeems man from the hopelessness which comes with his realization that he cannot alter the past, or change his past mistakes. For even though he cannot change the past, he achieves a kind of immortality, and every good act of his-both past and future-will be repeated over and over again, taking on an infinite value.

Acceptance of this doctrine, however, is not easy, because it also requires that one accept all the weaknesses of man, since they, too, recur eternally. It is necessary, therefore, to overcome disgust and loathing for man, as well as pity for man. Zarathustra was unable consciously to express this doctrine until he overcame his own disgust and pity (in The Convalescent).

This doctrine is open to more than one objection. First, it is not certain that the universe is infinite in extent. Some scientific theories assert just the opposite. The number of theoretical questions which still exist in this sphere make it difficult to reach any decision in the matter. But the "**metaphysical**" question (whether there is or is not such recurrence) is of secondary importance. Even if there were eternal recurrence, a person only experiences his own acts, and therefore the "immortality" which the doctrine offers has little meaning. The basic value of the doctrine, however, lies in its forceful command that all life should be affirmed, that every moment should be considered precious, as though it had infinite value. The highest affirmation of life is the willingness to ask for it all over again-in exactly the same way. Accepting the doctrine of eternal recurrence, then, is a way of expressing this extreme positive attitude toward life, and also a guide to future actions-shape your future so that you would be willing to repeat it. At the same time, it is a complete rejection of nihilistic pessimism, because it requires the acceptance of mistakes and weaknesses without regret.

Question: What is the "prejudice of opposites"? Give some of Nietzsche's own views that exemplify his rejection of this prejudice.

Answer: The prejudice of opposites has two forms: a **metaphysical** form and a moral form. In its **metaphysical** form, it is the belief that the universe contains distinct realms of being, which have no relationship at all to one another; for example, the realm of value and the realm of fact. In its moral form, it is the belief that every moral extreme has a contradictory opposite; for example, that whatever is unqualifiedly good has as its opposite that which is unqualifiedly bad. To complete the prejudice, there is added the belief that nothing can ever arise out of its opposite. This renders it impossible, for example, for value to grow out of the world of factual experience. In this way, the prejudice of opposites supports the view that values must be imposed upon things from a supernatural source (a view which Nietzsche rejects).

Nietzsche wholly repudiates this prejudice, and he shows this in several ways. In *Beyond Good and Evil*, he suggests that conscious thought is not opposed to instinctive behavior, but may even be a form of such behavior. This view is contrary to the traditional philosophical view that thought is entirely an action of the "mind," which can never arise out of the instincts, since they represent "body," which is opposed to "mind" (mind-body dualism). In other places, Nietzsche affirms that spirituality and sexuality are not opposed, that free will and necessity are interdependent, and that benevolence can grow out of a true selfishness. All of these reflect his thoroughgoing antipathy toward the prejudice of opposites.

Question: What, according to Nietzsche, is the ultimate significance of the ascetic ideal?

Answer. The ascetic ideal is the doctrine which esteems, above all else, poverty, humility, and chastity. This ideal, Nietzsche says, has had a widespread acceptance. This acceptance is paradoxical, because these ideals are contrary to the perpetuation of life itself. Nietzsche does not believe that would man knowingly accept an ideal which leads him to self-destruction, and he therefore seeks for the ultimate meaning of the ascetic ideal in its ability to sustain life. Normally, such an ideal would not support life. But in a sick society, one which is weary of life and which has found all ideals lacking, the ascetic ideal can arise as the only possible ideal that can succeed. It is one ideal which can give meaning to a life in which all other hope of meaning has been lost. By making the very element which destroys other ideals (sickness) into the essence of the new ideal, a lasting goal is achieved. Such an ideal, however, can be of value only to a sick society. It is, in fact, no more than a desire for "nothingness," and therefore it is an extreme measure. But Nietzsche points out that man will only survive if he has something to desire, and he would rather desire nothingness, if the only alternative is to have no desire, no will, at all.

Nietzsche symbolizes this willingness to worship anything rather than have no object of worship, in the passage titled The Ass Festival, in *Thus Spoke Zarathustra* (in which the "higher men" worship the ass, having realized that "God is dead"). Nietzsche, of course, does not advocate the ascetic ideal. He believes that man must give life a meaning which is life-affirming, not life-negating. In order to do this, however, man must change his idea of the sort of meaning which life requires in order to be worthwhile. He must abandon the idea that life is meaningless unless there are absolute truths and fixed moral values. Only then will he be able to give life a man-made meaning, through the creation of values. The man who can do this is the "Superman" of the future, represented by Zarathustra.

BIBLIOGRAPHY

TEXTS

Nietzsche, F. *The Birth of Tragedy* and *The Genealogy of Morals*, translated by Francis Golffing; Doubleday and Company, New York, 1956 (Anchor A-81).

Nietzsche, F. *Thus Spoke Zarathustra*, translated, with an introduction, by R. J. Hollingdale; Penguin Books, Baltimore, 1961 (Penguin L118).

Nietzsche, F. *Beyond Good and Evil*, translated by Helen Zimmern; in *The Philosophy of Nietzsche*, Random House, New York, 1927 (Modern Library Giant G34). Also contains translations of *Thus Spoke Zarathustra*, *The Genealogy of Morals*, *Ecce Homo*, and *The Birth of Tragedy*.

COMMENTARIES AND RELATED TEXTS

Campbell, J. *The Hero with a Thousand Faces*, Meridian Books, New York, 1956 (M22).

Jung, C. G. *Psyche and Symbol*, Doubleday and Company, New York, 1958 (Anchor A-136).

Kaufmann, W. *Existentialism from Dostoevsky to Sartre*, Meridian Books, New York, 1957 (M39).

Kaufmann, W. *Nietzsche: Philosopher, Psychologist, Antichrist*. World Publishing Co., New York, 1956 (Meridian M25).

Manthey-Zorn, O. *Nietzsche*. Washington Square Press, New York, 1964 (W594).

Morgan, G. A. Jr. *What Nietzsche Means*; Harvard University Press, Cambridge, Mass., 1941.

BEYOND GOOD AND EVIL

KEY TO IMPORTANT PASSAGES

TOPIC: THE SUPERMAN

REFER TO

Thus Spoke Zarathustra

Zarathustra's Prologue (Comment) Of Marriage and Children (Comment) Of Voluntary Death (Comment) Of the Blissful Isles (Comment) Of the Great Longing Of the Higher Man The Intoxicated Song

Beyond Good and Evil:

Sections 210-211, 270-274.

The Genealogy of Morals:

Second Essay, Section 24.

TOPIC: THE WILL TO POWER

REFER TO

Thus Spoke Zarathustra:

Of the Thousand and one Goals Of Self-overcoming (Comment)

Beyond Good and Evil:

Sections 211, 229-231.

TOPIC: ETERNAL RECURRENCE

REFER TO

Thus Spoke Zarathustra:

Of Redemption (Comment) Of the Vision and the Riddle The Convalescent At Noontide (Comment) The Intoxicated Song (Comment)

Beyond Good and Evil:

Section 56.

TOPIC: SELF-OVERCOMING (SUBLIMATION)

REFER TO

The Birth of Tragedy:

Section titled "Beauty in Art"

Thus Spoke Zarathustra:

Of the Tree on the Mountainside Of the Thousand and one Goals (Comment) Of the Three Metamorphoses The Bestowing Virtue (Comment) Of Self-overcoming Of the Sublime Men The Wanderer (Comment)

Beyond Good and Evil:

Sections 188-189, 295.

The Genealogy of Morals:

Second Essay, Sections 1-3.

TOPIC: REALITY AND KNOWLEDGE

REFER TO

Thus Spoke Zarathustra:

Of Immaculate Perception (Comment) Of the Afterworldsmen

Beyond Good and Evil:

Sections 2, 4, 23, 24, 34-38, 192-193, 210-211.

> **TOPIC: NIHILISM**

> **REFER TO**

Thus Spoke Zarathustra:

Of the Despisers of the Body (Comment) Of the Vision and the Riddle (Comment) Of the Spirit of Gravity

Beyond Good and Evil:

Sections 210-211 (Comment)

The Genealogy of Morals:

Second Essay, Sections 19-21. Third Essay, Sections 15-22 (Comment).